What others are sayir

David Fessenden's *Writing the (*
Contract* is must reading for every Christian writer who hopes to one
day get a book in print. David's practical advice is presented clearly and
sprinkled with humor. Highly readable and highly recommended!

— **Marlene Bagnull**, Litt.D., Director, Colorado and Greater
Philadelphia Christian Writers Conferences. Author of *Write His
Answer: A Bible Study for Christian Writers.*

* * *

With a friendly, engaging voice, Dave Fessenden invites us behind the
mysterious veil of creating a publishable book. His step-by-step process
describes what pros already know: researching, outlining, and proposal
writing come before drafting and revising. As in any work we undertake,
only preparation and planning will lead us to our goal—in this case, seeing
our books in readers' hands. For more than a decade I've known Dave as
editor, fellow author, and friend. Let his practical, real-world book lead
you on your own fantastic journey toward publication.

— **Julie-Allyson Ieron**, author of *The Overwhelmed Woman's Guide
to... Caring for Aging Parents* (Moody), and *The Julie-Allyson
Ieron Bible Reference Collection* (Wordsearch Bible Software),
www.joymediaservices.com

* * *

Dave Fessenden's book, *Writing the Christian Nonfiction Book: Concept to
Contract*, is a "God-send" to the well-intentioned but sometimes unsure
author who has a burning idea but doesn't know how to transfer desire
into the nuts-and-bolts process of getting a book published. Whether you
are a seasoned author or a novice, this book takes you through the process
start to finish. It can be the difference between success and frustration!
I recommend it wholeheartedly!

— **Harold J. Sala**, Ph.D., Founder and President of Guidelines
International, www.guidelines.org, author of 46 books

* * *

From the first waves of brainstorming to writing the proposal and
then landing a contract, David Fessenden provides clear, logical
and practical steps for anyone with a non-fiction book idea. I first
encountered these concepts at a writing workshop taught by Mr.
Fessenden and it inspired me with a can-do attitude. Rolling through
his writing cycle gives fluidity to the project and wings to your idea.

Writing the Christian Nonfiction Book: Concept to Contract is a must for the nonfiction writer.

— **Jeanne Doyon**, Freelance Writer/Speaker, www.streams-edge.blogspot. com. Her articles have appeared in *Evangel, Live, Proverbs 31 Magazine,* and her story, "Late Bloomer," is included in *Kisses of Sunshine for Women* by Thelma Wells and Carol Kent.

* * *

Dave's book clearly lays out the necessary elements of a complete plan for the writing cycle, spiced with doses of both reality and encouragement. This book gives a clear explanation of the elements that make up that plan. It has been useful to stir me to consider ways to improve the book I am now working on. I had gotten to the point where I felt that I was micromanaging the process endlessly. Now I have some specific ideas as to what to look for.

— **William Shumway**, attorney and writer

* * *

This is "Vintage Dave Fessenden": witty, non-threatening, and extremely helpful. Dave has the rare quality of being able to talk us through our foibles as writers while cheering us on to success. As an editor and an author himself, he is uniquely qualified to guide us, step-by- step, in creating manuscripts worthy of publication. This is solid and sensitive mentoring at its best!

— **Joyce Strong**, International speaker, joycestrongministries.org; author of *Lambs on the Ledge; Caught in the Crossfire; Instruments for His Glory; Leading with Passion and Grace; Journey to Joy; Of Dreams and Kings and Mystical Things;* and *A Dragon, a Dreamer and the Promise Giver.*

* * *

Helpful, humorous, and honest, *Concept to Contract* is more like a comprehensive conversation on conceiving and crafting a quality book than a stiff, starchy how-to-write-a-book book. Laced with great quotations and personal anecdotes, it's easy to follow and fun to read. Don't be misled, however: although this book eschews pedantic pedagogy, it delivers on its promise to clarify the process of crafting a concept so that it lands a contract. Thanks, Dave, for sharing these insider secrets!

— **Patti Souder**, Director of Montrose Christian Writers Conference. She is the author of four books, teaches writing at Davis College, and co-hosts a radio program with her husband Larry.

WRITING THE CHRISTIAN NONFICTION BOOK:

CONCEPT TO CONTRACT

Dear Adrienne,
May the Lord guide you in
your writing efforts!

David E Fessenden

DAVID E. FESSENDEN

SONFIRE MEDIA
A PUBLISHING COMPANY
GALAX, VIRGINIA

Writing the Christian Nonfiction Book: Concept to Contract

Published by Sonfire Media, LLC
411 N. Main Street
Galax, VA 24333 USA

Original illustrations created by Ed VanDeMark
Cover and interior book design by Larry W. Van Hoose

ISBN No. 978-0-9825773-3-2

To Sandy Brooks and Vie Herlocker

Sandy, thanks for believing in me and for publishing the "Editor's Soapbox" column in *The Cross & Quill*, from which much of this book is derived. Your encouragement has helped me accomplish more than I ever thought possible.

Vie, your work as editor of this book was outstanding! You cleaned out the clichés, hunted down the repetitive wording (yes, I do say "a lot" a lot!), and graciously but frankly pointed out when I was being obtuse. I really appreciate it.

> "And let us consider how we may spur one another on toward love and good deeds." (Hebrews 10:24)

Contents

Foreword
by Leonard G. Goss

The condition of American publishing being what it is today, the chances of being published are next to nil unless your material is as good as it can be. Even very good manuscripts sometimes cannot land a publisher. Why? Bookwork is done on a priority basis, and publishing houses are not going to spend peoplepower and money on writing that falls below a very high standard, or on books that cost more than they sell. Why should they? They have to determine which books are more vital to their well-being, and that means deciding what few books see the light of day, and what amount of attention is given to each book on their list. Beyond that, Christian publishers also want to see books that help readers discover what this life is for. Naturally, the better the book is, the more a publisher is willing to take it on.

There is no room for writing that is less than the best. The poet William Carlos Williams warns, "It is dangerous to leave written that which is badly written. A chance word, upon paper, may destroy the world. Watch carefully and erase, while the power is still yours . . . for all that is put down, once it escapes, may rot its way into a thousand minds, the corn become a black smut, and all libraries, of necessity, be burned to the ground as a consequence" (*Paterson*). Words *mean* something, so beware of them. They are far too powerful and important *not* to take them seriously. They are a divine gift and powerful tools in the hands of good writers.

A book may be inert, but what happens in the mind of someone who reads a good book is electric. Emily Dickinson went on many travels in her lifetime, but she almost never left her home. She wrote, "There is no Frigate like a Book / To take us lands away / Nor any Coursers like a page / Of Prancing Poetry./ This Traverse may the poorest take /

Without oppress of Toll— / How frugal is the Chariot / That bears the Human Soul" (*There is no Frigate like a Book*). Are you interested in writing that bears the human soul? Are you interested in writing that reveals the very heart and core of the story of God? Then you must prepare.

Here is how: Pray (1 Thess. 5:17). Wait on God (Ps. 37:7). Keep your eyes on Christ (Heb. 12:2). Read Scripture (John 5:39). Besides Scripture, be a wide reader. Write with passion, purity, and power, and believe you can make a difference. Put on the full armor of God (Eph. 6:11-13). Ask God to give you a vision for your writing (Prov. 29:18). Write things that have to do with spiritual values and spiritual growth. Bring out your best writing to share the world's best message of hope. Forgo the jackpot syndrome (Prov. 11:28). Pursue and uncover truth (Ps. 86:11). Develop discernment. Strike a blow for the Kingdom. Be *in* the world but not *of* it (John 17:14-18). Proclaim freedom (Luke 4:18) and the year of the Lord's favor (Luke 4:19). And become equipped for writing and publishing by finding good resources.

Now all of this means you want to make your written material as good as it can be. To do that one needs excellent writing resources, and that brings us to Dave Fessenden's *Writing the Christian Nonfiction Book: Concept to Contract*. This book is no armchair guide alone. It is a valuable text to take in hand for teachers of expository writing. As such, it is a concrete, sound, and honest introduction to writing and publishing Christian nonfiction. It is foremost, however, an excellent inside perspective for writers serious about understanding the confusing and mysterious maze that is nonfiction book publishing. More than that, it is a soup-to-nuts survey of the craft of writing and getting that writing commercially published. My favorite chapters are the ones on research, front-end book proposals, and fine-tuning the manuscript.

It contains many helpful facts, but the primary purpose of this book is to stimulate thinking and help readers understand how research and writing is to be done, and how to muster the resources needed to do it. The guidance is solid and the advice is concise, easily applied, and often entertaining. This primer is one of the best and most helpful how-to books available in its field. Dave Fessenden's more-than-worthwhile book will benefit readers at all levels.

Books will be with us for a long time to come. In a lecture sponsored by the Center for the Book in the Library of Congress, historian Barbara Tuchman said that "Books are the carriers of civilization. Without books, history is silent, literature dumb, science crippled, thought and speculation at a standstill. Without books, the development of civilization would have been impossible. They are the engines of change, windows on the world, and lighthouses erected in the sea of time. They are companions, teachers, magicians, bankers of the treasure of the mind. Books are humanity in print." And specifically Christian writing and publishing will be with us for a long time to come because God wants and uses books. In other words, the welfare of the church depends on the welfare of books and reading. Christians must read. We are the people of the Book. If we are to read, then we must also write. Here is a book to get you going.

Leonard G. Goss

www.goodeditors.com

Author of *The Little Style Guide to Great Christian Writing and Publishing* and *The Little Handbook to Perfecting the Art of Christian Writing: Getting Your Foot in the Publisher's Door*

CHAPTER 1

THE MYSTERIOUS PROCESS

Unprovided with original learning, unformed in the habits of thinking, unskilled in the arts of composition, I resolved to write a book.

— Edward Gibbon
author of *The Decline and Fall of the Roman Empire*

It took me fifteen years to discover I had no talent for writing, but I couldn't give it up because by that time I was too famous.

— Robert Benchley

W. Somerset Maugham said, "There are three rules for writing the novel. Unfortunately, no one knows what they are."

Though Maugham was speaking about fiction, the truth behind his wisecrack applies just as well to nonfiction. It's true—to some extent, the process of writing a book is a mystery worthy of Sherlock Holmes.

I've written and contributed to several books, and each one was a unique project, with its own unique issues, problems, and solutions.

This is as it should be. A writer who learns how to crank out books like so many sausages will end up with manuscripts that *read* like sausages. But more important than that is the fact that any good book is the result of inspiration, followed by hours of grueling work.

I don't know about you, but for me, inspiration is not a problem (except that it comes at the most inconvenient times, doesn't it?). It's the prospect of the hard work that gets to me—it shuts down my brain, wiping away any shred of creativity. No wonder most authors have no idea where to begin when they sit down to write a book.

The Inward Pressure

As a Christian writer, your understanding of the mystery of inspiration is all the more deep and profound. "The only book that should ever be written," said A.W. Tozer, "is one that flows up from the heart, forced out by the inward pressure. When such a work has gestated within a man it is almost certain that it will be written." [1]

Perhaps you are feeling that "inward pressure" but you are looking for the right starting point. If so, I think I can help.

Maybe you've already started but are stuck. If you're anything like me, you probably have several, if not dozens, of writing projects that are in various stages of completion: half-done, in rough outline, or still no farther along than a collection of ideas scratched out on scraps of paper. The only time you ever seem to get anything done is during those rare and beautiful periods of creative momentum—the words are flowing, the structure of the piece is clear, and there are no distractions. (Deadlines imposed by others can work as well—there's nothing quite so motivating as an editor screaming, "Where's that manuscript?")

But rather than waiting for a perfect alignment of the electrons in your body (or whatever it is that causes those rare periods of unhindered output), you can keep a project moving ahead if you pay attention to the dynamics of what I call "the writing cycle"—the natural progression of a writing project from concept to completion.

In the following pages I will show you eight steps—or eight elements, anyway—that will make the process a little less mystical. These are roughly chronological, yet you will find that you may do them a bit out of order, or even do two or more of them simultaneously:

1. Brainstorming
2. Researching
3. Outlining
4. Preparing the Proposal
5. Writing the Rough Draft
6. Revising
7. Fine-tuning the Manuscript
8. Getting the Contract

Let's go over these one at a time:

1. Brainstorming

The process of developing the idea, coming up with related concepts, and putting these thoughts down on paper is called brainstorming.

Don't worry about organizing or judging the merits of your material at this point. Have fun with this part! Brainstorming is the topic of chapter two.

2. Researching

Once you've done your brainstorming, you may think it's time to prepare an outline. Whoa there, sport. The next step is to verify, broaden, and enhance your ideas by conducting research.

In research, there are two main storehouses of information: public (library, Internet, books, etc.), and private (compiling your own ideas and knowledge, and interviewing others). The Internet can be great for research, but don't let it be a crutch. We discuss this in chapter three.

3. Outlining

You'll use the notes from your brainstorming and research to create an outline. Many writers avoid this step for fear of coming up with something artificial. Such a fear is groundless. You don't need to create the kind of symmetrical outline that would have made your grade-school English teacher proud. The purpose of an outline is to map out the project in a way that works for you. We'll cover this in chapter four.

4. Preparing the Proposal

A *book proposal* is the tool used to sell a book to a publisher . Some writers may wonder why I put this step here. Shouldn't proposal writing occur after you complete a final version of your manuscript? Absolutely not! If you wait until then, your energy level for the project is so low that you are less likely to do a good selling job. "Please buy my manuscript; I'm sick of looking at it" is not a convincing argument. Besides, in preparing to sell the idea to an editor, I often find myself asking questions about the project that I missed when I was brainstorming and outlining: Who is the audience? What is the main point of the manuscript? What is the take-away value for the reader? We'll talk about proposal components in chapter five.

5. Writing the Rough Draft

Believe me, this is just what it sounds like—a *rough* draft. It's not a masterpiece; in some cases, it may be little more than an expanded outline. Writing the rough draft can be a much more pleasant experience if you decide that your goal is to get words on paper (or on the computer screen), and not to achieve perfection. We wrestle with perfectionism, as well as other writers' neuroses, in chapter six.

6. Revising

Rewriting, revising, and trimming the draft into something approximating a completed manuscript is what we're talking about here. This is where the *real* writing starts. (And if the revisions are extensive enough, you may discover you need to revise the book proposal at this stage, as well. Isn't this *fun*?) That's the subject of chapter seven.

7. Fine-Tuning the Manuscript

The manuscript must be fine-tuned before submission. Fine-tuning means checking page numbers, your name and address on each page, endnotes, permissions, etc.—all the little details necessary to ready the manuscript for submission. Like outlining, this step is often skipped or done poorly, and many manuscripts are rejected for this reason alone. We'll look at how to avoid those rejection slips in chapter eight.

8. Getting the Contract

Obtaining a contract is the goal you hope to attain by sending the proposal and/or the manuscript to publishing houses for consideration. Perhaps an editor has already seen your proposal at a writers' conference or some other venue, and is waiting to see the full manuscript. Lucky you! But if your brilliant masterpiece is still undiscovered, and you're feeling like the entrances to publishing houses are locked and barred to you, there are methods for storming the gates. This process is covered in chapter nine.

Often I find that when I am stuck on a project, it is the result of not spending enough time in one of the steps. For example, if I am having trouble writing my first draft, perhaps I haven't worked hard enough on the proposal to keep me motivated. Or maybe I haven't clearly outlined the project. Maybe I even need to go back to doing some brainstorming, because I haven't clearly thought out the point of the book I am writing.

Remember that the order in which you perform these eight steps is up to you. I jump around a lot with the steps, and I find that they feed on each other. For example, maybe I'm fine-tuning the manuscript (step seven), and something about it just isn't working right. Of course, I'll review the rewriting I did (step six); perhaps I deleted some essential information. I will check my rough draft (step five) to see if I can find where the problem originated. I may even look over my book proposal (step four)—especially if an editor has shown some interest. Maybe the final version doesn't deliver what I promised in the proposal—no wonder I'm stuck! And that means I should go back to rethinking my outline (step three), or even doing some more research (step two) and brainstorming (step one).

With all this backtracking over previous steps, does a project *ever* get out of the writing cycle? That is the reason for step eight. The editor is not going to come to your house and pull the manuscript from your white-knuckled hands. You have to come to a point where you say, "Well, it isn't perfect, but it's the best I can do," and you send it off with a prayer that God will honor your diligence.

That's when you get to step nine—celebrate! You've completed the task God has called you to do and you've put it in His hands. If the manuscript is accepted and published, that's just icing on the cake.

I've just shared the basic process for writing a book, and it's easier than it sounds—especially because I intend to show you some professional secrets that keep things moving along. I can't guarantee that it's foolproof (fools can be so unpredictable), but I can promise that this process will work, if you stick to it with diligence.

I know one foolproof method, however. Here's how *not* to write a book: You come up with the grain of an idea, write several pages of a first chapter, then stuff it in a folder and never look at it again. I have *several* books like that!

If you really want to produce a complete, publishable manuscript, you need to pray a lot, think a lot, study a lot, research a lot—and do very little actual *writing* at first. Research, outlining, and preparing the proposal should build up a creative pressure in you that demands an outlet—so that the book practically writes itself. Yeah, right. But at least it'll be a little easier.

Collector or Craftsman?

Let me close with an excerpt from an article by Larry Libby, which illustrates the difference between two kinds of writers:

> My father-in-law, Bob, doesn't have many tools.
>
> Half of what he owned got lifted out of the back of his pickup on a mean street in Sacramento. He's mislaid several more, and worn out a few of his favorites through merciless use. But it doesn't really matter. When you're a determined fix-it guy, you just find a way.
>
> Give Bob a hammer, a screwdriver, a pair of pliers, and a can of WD-40, and he'll take on the world. No household repair job is too daunting, from a clogged toilet to a bulky thermostat to a leaky roof . . . .

I have another friend who has more tools than the Ace Hardware man. Wrenches of all proportions hang over his workbench in gleaming steely splendor. Drill bits ranging from the radius of a toothpick to the girth of a small tree grace the pegboard in flawless ascending order . . . .

But, it's funny. Try as I might, I can't think of anything my friend has actually built or repaired. I can't remember ever seeing him *use* those marvelous tools he's collected. . . .

My friend Al Janssen recently finished a stint as a featured teacher at a writer's conference. A gifted writer, editor, and publisher, Al had decided that the best way to teach some of his time-tested techniques was to get the conferees into the act. In two days of training, he led them in the use of four of his patented writing tools. Knowing Al, I have no doubt that the experience was akin to trailing Teddy Roosevelt on a charge up San Juan Hill.

"Sure, I put 'em to work," Al said. "I wanted them to go home with some practical experience as well as four shiny new tools."

But not everyone appreciated my friend's storm-the-hill approach. One angry woman cornered him at the end of his final session. This was *not* what she had expected. She had come prepared to listen and absorb and take careful notes. She was *most* disappointed by the "lack of content."

To her way of thinking, a writers' conference meant sitting in a comfortable chair, sipping a cup of herbal tea, and basking in the rarefied presence of "real" authors and editors. That someone might actually expect her to *write* something was simply contemptible.

My friend felt a little chastened by the rebuke until the lady added, "Furthermore, this is my *fourth* writing conference this year, and *none* of the teachers have asked us to do anything like this!"

Al suddenly understood. She was a tool collector. Some people gather tools. Some people use the ones they have. The quantity of work you accomplish is not necessarily proportionate to the number of tools you possess.[2]

Take your choice: do you want to be a tool collector or a craftsman? If you're ready to break a sweat, get your hands dirty, and hone your skills to see that book through to completion, just turn the page.

CHAPTER 2

BRAINSTORMING: CORRALLING YOUR IDEAS

Great ideas need landing gear as well as wings.

— C. D. Jackson

The above quote is a very perceptive description of brainstorming. Jackson's point is that we need to ponder all aspects of an idea before we try to implement it—the same way that an aeronautical engineer should design a plane to not only get up in the air, but also safely back to earth.

If you think about it, very few of your usable ideas come to you full-blown; even the best of them are rough until you refine and streamline them. I've found that I cannot bring an idea to maturity until I deliberately take it past the embryonic stage—the "Eureka!" moment that we all have once in a while. If a writer runs with an idea at the "Eureka!" stage, it often either loses steam or produces mediocre results. The idea wasn't developed to the point of implementation. The way to get to that point with an idea is to take it through the brainstorming process, where every facet of the idea is analyzed and applied to real life. This is how to give your ideas "landing gear."

Ether Dreams and Great Ideas

H. Allen Smith tells an interesting story of Oliver Wendell Holmes Sr., father of the famous jurist and a respected author and physician. It seems Holmes was put under ether while doing some medical experimentation with anesthesia. As he began to lose consciousness, a great idea came to him. He immediately realized he had stumbled on the answer to mankind's greatest problems. This great idea, if properly implemented, would solve all poverty, end all wars, and bring about an era of utopia.

Unfortunately, when he awoke from the ether, Holmes could not recall the great idea. In desperation, he convinced one of his colleagues to put him under again, this time with a stenographer in the room. His plan was to speak the great idea aloud. The stenographer would write it down for posterity. As the ether began to take effect, the great idea, now seemingly more wonderful than before, filled his mind. Holmes opened his mouth and spoke these immortal words: "The entire universe is permeated with the smell of turpentine."

Most of us have probably experienced the same kind of disappointment that Holmes must have felt after he woke up from the anesthesia. It can be painfully discouraging when an idea that seemed to be gold turns out to be straw. Sometimes an idea seems to write itself. Other times you feel like your creativity is trying to run with a sprained ankle. Is an idea more inspired by God because it flows freely? Not necessarily. Sometimes it is deeper or more complex, and that is why it is hard work. But sometimes you're trying to capitalize on an idea with an inherent flaw, and instead of *capitalizing*, you should be *euthanizing*!

What constitutes a good idea? How do you judge whether an idea is good, or just an ether dream?

The Power of a Compelling Idea

In publishing, nothing beats the power of a compelling idea. It is important to develop your writing skill and prepare a thorough and well-done proposal—but many writers have published their first book based on the flimsiest of proposals. Here is what makes the difference: the power of a compelling idea.

What makes a good idea? A truly compelling idea has to ride the line between being commonplace and eclectic. On the one hand, it has to be distinctive, not something a million articles and books have already been written about. It's impossible, of course, to be entirely original. Ecclesiastes 1:9 says there is nothing new under the sun. As Josh Billings pointed out (with tongue placed firmly in cheek), "About the most originality that any writer can hope to achieve is to steal with good judgment." It's fine to get an idea from another person, but you must strive for distinctiveness in what you do with that idea. You must make it your own.

On the other hand, is your idea so distinctive that it is eclectic? Is it so esoteric, so idiosyncratic, so downright *weird* that nobody understands what you mean? Is it so bizarre that no one can relate to it? How do you get the right balance?

A first step is to get to know yourself. What are the things that make your walk with God unique? What aspects of your walk with God do you have in common with others? *It is where those two things intersect that you find your ideas.*

For example, I picked up one article idea from my mother, who has a knack for describing things in unusual ways. One day as we walked out of church, she turned to me and said, "Sometimes I feel like the third verse of a hymn." Immediately I knew what she meant. In our church, we sometimes skip the third verse of a hymn if the service is running late. "I feel like the third verse of a hymn" was Mom's way of saying she felt left out. My mother's unique ability at description was intersecting with her very common problem of feeling lonely. This was a great germ of an idea for an article, which I later sold to *Power for Living.*

I have had unusual experiences. For example, I have been a newspaper reporter, a profession specializing in gathering voluminous information, carefully picking out the most important, and putting it down on paper in an interesting and readable format—all done with a daily deadline. I found that the techniques I learned as a reporter and in my college journalism courses can be applied very easily to Christian writing—even fiction. So I put them into a workshop called "Journalistic Techniques in Christian Writing," which I have presented at Christian writers' conferences.

The uniqueness/sameness concept runs through most every piece of writing—even jokes. Humor often hinges on uniqueness and sameness. Bill Cosby takes a unique situation in his life and exaggerates it out of proportion for comic effect. But what makes his humor so lovable is that there is sameness to it—we can identify with at least part of the most unusual, exaggerated stories he tells.

Another thing about a good idea, one that comes from the Lord, is that it will survive analysis; it will survive criticism; it will survive putting it on the shelf for a couple weeks. A good idea will even survive prayer.

Oliver Wendell Holmes' idea did *not* survive analysis—but maybe yours will. And if not, you are the most blessed of souls, for you have not wasted your time on an ether dream. Put the idea aside, and then move on. Are you willing to let your pet project die if the Lord wants it to die?

How exactly do you analyze an idea? One place to begin is at its roots. When you get an idea, ask yourself how or when you thought of it. The roots of an idea can show you where to further refine and streamline it. If you think about it, very few of your usable ideas come to you full-blown; most need to cook for a while. In my own experience, I've found that I cannot bring an idea to maturity until I walk it through the following stages:

1. Initial conception of the idea—the Eureka! moment that we all have once in a while

2. Brainstorming every facet of the idea, and how the idea applies to real life

3. Researching and testing related ideas, pondering the problems, checking out the competition

4. Organizing the various aspects of the idea into some sort of order, as a prelude to writing about it

Often a writer runs with an idea at the initial conception stage and either loses steam or produces mediocre results. The idea usually wasn't developed to the point of implementation. You can get to that point with an idea, but it takes some work. Sit down and brainstorm it—write down all aspects of the idea as they come. There are several ways to do brainstorming. Here are a few that have worked for others, and for me:

1. Webbing or Bubble Charting

In the center of a blank sheet of paper, write your basic idea in as few words as possible. Draw a circle (a "bubble") around the idea. Think of a related idea, write it down, and put it in its own bubble. Draw a line from the first bubble to the second. As you continue to brainstorm ideas, create more bubbles and draw lines between them and other related ideas. Don't be afraid to draw multiple lines to express more complex relationships between ideas. You may end up seeing how your fifth idea, though related to your fourth idea, also has a direct connection to your second idea; draw another line to represent that relationship. You may need to label the lines to remind yourself what the relationship is; for example, love is related to fear through 1 John 4:18 ("perfect love drives out fear"). Work on the chart until you have created a complex web of connections. My son used this method to brainstorm a novel he was writing—using sheets of newsprint about four feet square!

2. Index Cards

Many people like to write out their ideas in more detail, and index cards work very well. This is *not* the use of index cards that you may have been taught in school, where you carefully write out the full text and citation of a quote for use in a research paper. Your notes don't have to be neat and tidy; they don't even have to make sense to anyone but you. When you have written out several ideas, label each card with its own letter, number, or symbol (some people like to use symbols— !, @, #, $, %, ^, &, *—because letters or numbers may subconsciously influence them to put the cards in a certain order, so that they tend to ignore interrelationships). Spread out the cards and review your ideas. Write the letter, number, or symbol from one card onto another to identify a relationship. You may need to write notes on the cards (maybe on the back) to help you remember the relationships.

3. "Sticky" Notes

I once met a technical writer named Dave Young who shared this method with me—a variation on the index card technique. He put his ideas on self-stick notepaper and slapped them onto the nearest wall. Then he rearranged them to find the interrelationships. He called it his "off-the-wall" approach to brainstorming.

4. Stream-of-Consciousness Writing

This is my favorite. I just grab a legal pad and start writing my ideas down, talking it out on paper. When I come to a new idea, I separate it with a couple of blank lines. My notes may consist of single words, sentences, or paragraphs of varying lengths. Sometimes I will write two or three pages on a single idea. It's not great writing, nor is it always grammatically correct, but it gets the ideas down. When I review my notes, I simply write down interrelationships in the left margin of the page. (A word of warning: don't be like some authors, who think they can skip further stages in the writing process and simply write the whole book this way. Not only do they end up with a disjointed and disordered manuscript, but they may also find that they run out of steam after thirty pages or so.)

5. Audio Tape

More verbal people find it helpful to start a tape recorder and talk their ideas out. Then they review their ideas as they transcribe the tape. Other people are more social, more interactive, and they may have friends who are good listeners, and who know how to ask the right questions. They like to sit down over a cup of coffee and discuss their ideas with their friends—as they record the conversation.

A bad idea will not hold up under this kind of scrutiny, and reveals itself as an old, overused idea, clothed in different words. When this happens, the bad idea either fades away or—thank you, Lord!—transforms itself into a different, better idea. And a good idea will survive, and even thrive, on extensive brainstorming and research.

Another test of the worth of an idea is how easy it is to come up with a good title. A good idea can be encapsulated in a single sentence or phrase. This proves the idea is focused and clear enough to develop into a book. That's what editors mean when they say an idea isn't focused—it's not trimmed down to a single idea that is threaded throughout the entire manuscript. But if you've developed your ideas through disciplined brainstorming, you won't have that problem.

An idea must be developed, but sometimes the patient dies on the table. Mourn it briefly and get on with the next idea. (Just be thankful it died quickly; the devil wants you busy with worthless ideas so that you do not have time to follow up on God's ideas.)

Don't let your emotions cloud your judgment, however. Just because an idea tickles you is no proof it's good. And just because an idea seems to deflate when you first begin to brainstorm it is no proof it's bad. Pray for guidance. Praying about ideas is a way of sorting them out and finding God's will. Proverbs 16:9 says, "In his heart a man plans his course, but the Lord determines his steps."

Once you've done a healthy round of brainstorming, it may seem like a practical idea to start researching and outlining—maybe it's even time to start writing, right? Wrong! It seems counterintuitive, but many writers say that if they deliberately leave an idea alone for a while, it actually makes the creativity level increase.

Now is the time for a little creative goofing off. Don't be afraid to let an idea sit. Sleep on it. Let it cook. You will find that, without any effort on your part, your brain will start mulling over the concept and identify aspects of it that never came up in your earlier brainstorming session.

You'll also discover that, when left alone for a day or two, a bad idea is like a dead fish in the summer sun—it begins to stink. I have written down a number of ideas in the middle of the night that I thought were great, but in the cold light of day, I realized they were awful. That flash of excitement over an idea is deceptive. The next time you're tempted to dive into implementing an idea without giving it some time, remember Oliver Wendell Holmes and his "turpentine universe."

Adapting Ideas

Thorough brainstorming of an idea helps you adapt the idea to the appropriate medium. Is it really best suited for nonfiction? Is it a big enough idea to sustain itself through the multiple chapters of a book, or would it be better as an article or devotional? Do you see how difficult it is to answer such questions until you've fleshed out an idea with brainstorming and research? How can you know that an idea is book length until you've looked at all the aspects of it?

"Maybe you should write a book" is a common piece of advice you will hear as a writer. (There's even a book with that title.) But the hard truth is that everyone, it seems, has written a book and wants to publish it. And too many beginning writers secretly think they can bypass the normal learning process. They want to run before they can walk. In other words, the first thing they *ever* try to write and publish is a book-length manuscript.

The smart beginners hone their skills on magazine articles before they tackle a book-length project. I can't count the number of times I've read a book submission that was a terrible book, but would have made a great article.

Even if the idea is clearly nonfiction and obviously book length, there are many genres under the nonfiction umbrella. It is hard for most of us to decide on the appropriate genre because we tend to write in ruts. Some Christian writers, for example, do nothing but devotionals. Why? Because it's such a simple format: personal illustration, spiritual application, Scripture passage, and a prayer. Just like the old sermon—three points and a prayer! Now what happens if you come up with an idea that doesn't fit the devotional format? Do you reject it? Do you warp it to fit a devotional mold? Or do you try something new?

Problems Encountered with Ideas

If you have trouble evaluating your ideas, it may be because you don't know yourself that well. The uniqueness/sameness concept will be useless to you unless you have a good understanding of what makes you unique, and a good understanding of what you have in common with others. Think about your gifts and abilities, your weaknesses, your strengths. Pray that God will give you insight into how He made you, as well as how He is remaking you into Christ's image. Ask your friends what they like about you, what they were surprised to discover about you, what they have in common with you. All this makes great raw material for the idea maker between your ears.

Too many authors think they have unique ideas, but are blindly following the latest craze. Many of the submissions our publishing house receives are flagrant copies of popular books on the same subject by well-known Christian writers. After *The Purpose Driven Life* hit the best-seller lists, we got a load of manuscripts entitled

"Living Life on Purpose," "Having a Purpose in Your Life," and so on. *The Prayer of Jabez* was followed by "Applying the Jabez Prayer to Your Marriage/Family/Church," etc. Don't squander your gifts that way! You are a unique individual to whom God has given a unique message. Don't be a copy of anyone.

Other authors have the opposite problem—they think their ideas are too common, too ordinary; they figure that everything that could be written about the subject already has, so they never follow up on their ideas. And yet what seems common or ordinary to you may be a fresh insight to others. For example, I have struggled all my life with a certain weakness, and I know there is Scripture on the subject, so I figured there would be plenty of books and articles about it on the market. Guess what? There's almost nothing! One of these days I'm going to write an article about it.

The only solution to this is to bounce around ideas with other writers. Don't take every response to your idea as gospel, but weigh each one carefully. For example, don't let someone say to you, "Oh, nobody wants to read stories about animals." What about James Herriot's books?

Some ideas may be good, but they're not for you. For example, don't waste your time with historical material, a technical topic, or a biography if you are no good at and have no interest in *extensive* research. Why kill yourself? Ideas are a dime a dozen. Don't get riddled with guilt over all the ideas you can't follow up on. You want some ideas? I have a couple hundred scraps of paper with ideas— most have been done before (too much the same), or they are weird (too unusual).

Then again, maybe God wants to do a new thing in you. Don't reject an idea just because you've never done something like that before. Or worse, don't take an idea and twist it until it fits a genre or format you are used to. I've seen nonfiction ideas made into fiction, and article or chapter ideas made into devotionals—all because someone's too afraid to try something new.

Some ideas are shallow—a mile wide and an inch deep. As an editor, I regularly get manuscripts that claim to present the *whole* message of the *whole* Bible—in 160 pages! The books cover everything—a buckshot approach. Actually, what these writers are envisioning is a *survey* of the Bible, a kind of broad-brush commentary. It's not a bad idea, but so many others have already done it—and done it much better. Most readers are looking for something in-depth on a single subject, and that involves critical thinking and hard work.

In fact, that's a common thread in many bad ideas—they're too easy. I think that, unconsciously, we all tend to re-adapt our writing ideas to find the easy way out (after all, how often do you find yourself asking, "Isn't there a *harder* way to do this?"). We stick with formats we are familiar with, or we do a broad-brush approach on a subject because a narrow focus takes more work and requires more thought. We stay with familiar themes because we're afraid to try something new, or we are always looking for the most eclectic ideas we can find because we are afraid it's too hard to squeeze something fresh out of the more common and familiar.

Sometimes a good idea only seems bad because you have the wrong approach. But you can recycle ideas—making a bad idea into a good one by taking a different slant on it. Much of this chapter was a recycled idea. When I was asked to speak at a writer's conference one year, I suggested a workshop on the topic of creativity—what makes someone creative, etc. The topic was rejected and I'm glad it was. I was looking at this the wrong way. You see, I'm interested in the creative process because I'm an editor. Part of my job is finding and cultivating creative people. But you are a writer. The only person you're interested in being creative is *you*. I was caught up in a self-centered attitude—what interests me, instead of you, my audience. So I switched the focus around and concentrated on ideas and how to develop them—and here we are!

So there's another point of reference for refining an idea: is the concept oriented toward you or your audience?

The Battleground of Ideas

Finally, we should look at this whole topic from another perspective: something I call the battleground of ideas.

I get so many ideas I can't possibly implement them all. But if I believe that the Lord is superintending my writing ministry, and if I trust Him not to give me more work than I can get done, then I must accept that some of the ideas I get are from God, and others are not. So my job is to discern what is a gift from God and what is a "gift" from that un-holy trinity we are all so familiar with: the world, the flesh, and the devil. "Prove all things; hold fast to that which is good" (1 Thessalonians 5:21 KJV).

Have you considered that the creative process may involve spiritual warfare? The Lord gives ideas, but Satan gives ideas too—bad ideas and false ideas. Now a false idea—heresy or bad theology or a worldly outlook on a spiritual truth—should very quickly become evident to a Christian writer who is immersed in the Word. But bad ideas can be more subtle. Satan gives bad ideas—ones that are self-centered, that appeal to your pride—because he wants to waste your time. Satan would love to see you hyper-focused on an empty idea, and then lead you in the wrong direction—like a demonic GPS. That leaves you with no time to pursue the ideas God would have you work on—so readers out there somewhere don't read the book you *would* have written, and they continue to struggle when your book could have helped them.

OK, I'm really loading on the guilt, aren't I? But it's only to help you see that the pursuit of ideas is serious business, and not a pastime for spiritual dabblers. Every idea should be scrutinized by prayer. Inspiration and creativity are no proof of God's favor. The Tower of Babel was a creative project, but it sure didn't have God's approval.

The best ideas, I believe, are truly inspired by God. They may start out slow, but soon they gain momentum and develop a life of their own. And because God is sovereign, there is nothing you can do to "make" inspired ideas come. The only thing you can do is be faithful—be the kind of person that God can trust His ideas with. Be close to God, so you can hear when He speaks. Then you won't find yourself lost in an ether dream.

In your brainstorming, I hope you have surprised yourself, and discovered that you have more ideas than you thought you did. You have probably also seen a few weak spots (or even gaping holes) in your ideas. Now is the time to expand and strengthen those ideas through the process of research.

BRAINSTORMING TIP #1:

Ideas may come to you at the most inconvenient times, so make it a habit to carry a pocket notebook and pen. Then you can capture those flashes of brilliance before they get away!

BRAINSTORMING TIP #2:

Don't throw anything away! Some of the embryonic thoughts from your brainstorming notes may not find their way into your first draft, but could come in handy when you revise the manuscript or write sidebars.

BRAINSTORMING TIP #3:

Brainstorming is not done in one sitting. You may find yourself returning to this practice even after completing a first draft of the book.

CHAPTER 3

RESEARCH: PUBLIC AND PRIVATE

Therefore, since I myself have carefully investigated everything from the beginning, it seemed good also to me to write an orderly account for you. . . .

— Luke the Physician

A man will turn over half a library to make one book.

— Samuel Johnson

Once you've done your brainstorming, you may think it is time to prepare your outline. Yes, that sounds like a logical next step, but I want you to hold off on preparing an outline just now. If you prepare an outline at this point, I think you'll be disappointed with the results. Your brainstorming sessions have captured some good raw material for your book, but it's just that—*raw*. It needs to be refined; it is time to do *research*, in order to verify, broaden, and enhance your ideas.

Now don't panic. You may feel like you have to bushwhack your way through a jungle to research your ideas; however, there are only two main storehouses of information to sift through:

1. Private: yourself and others (delving into your own ideas, interviewing others)

2. Public: Internet, library, etc.

Private Research

Begin with *yourself* first. Review your brainstorming notes, sifting and digesting your own ideas on the topic. By analyzing, clarifying, and expanding your thoughts, you avoid the danger of simply parroting the ideas of others. Also, as you identify holes in your ideas or confusion about some aspect of the topic, it helps to know where to focus your research.

Private research of *others* can be individual (interviews) or corporate (surveys). Interviews and surveys (which are essentially interviewing multiple people with the same questions) are great ways to gather information. Your ideas can be fleshed out and made more rich and in-depth through the added input of other people. It is an active application of the proverb, "As iron sharpens iron, so one man sharpens another" (Proverbs 27:17).

You can conduct casual interviews and surveys by discussing your ideas with friends and acquaintances through e-mail and online social networks. There are times when you need specific expertise, and a face-to-face interview with an "expert" you have never met is almost unavoidable.

Most authors want to avoid interviewing because asking probing questions of a stranger can be scary. You can defuse the tension with a little preliminary research on the interviewee and topic to be discussed (what I call *public* research, which we'll talk about later). A knowledgeable interviewer—one who has done enough preliminary research about the subject to ask intelligent questions—sets the interviewee at ease, causes them to open up, and gives them the opportunity to go into more depth.

A Foolproof Method of Interviewing

If you write any amount of nonfiction, it's inevitable—at some point you're going to have to conduct an interview. And the only thing as intimidating as fielding questions is asking them. What if you freeze? What if your mind goes blank? What if you ask a stupid question and your interviewee laughs in your face?

Not to worry. You are a professional. You are cool under fire. And you are prepared to meet your intended victim with the five Ws—Who, What, Where, When, and Why. You have everything you need, right?

Wrong.

By the time you go into an interview, you had better already know the answers to the basic "five Ws." If you waste someone's time gathering information you could have obtained before the interview, you may be destined to receive that proverbial laugh in the face—and you are unlikely to receive a second interview.

For example, if you interview a historian on the battle of Gettysburg, you waste time asking the dates, number of troops, casualties, and other statistics and basic facts that can be gleaned from public sources. Here is a person who has spent years studying and pondering over *why* the battle occurred and its significance in the outcome of the war, and you waste this opportunity gathering facts you could have gotten from an encyclopedia. You even risk making the interviewee angry.

There is a better strategy for getting at the heart of a story: bring a GOAT to your next interview.

No, I don't mean a billy goat, I mean a GOAT—

Goal

Obstacles

Answers

Time

GOAT is an interview method based on the idea that life is a series of conflicts, a series of episodes with a protagonist (your interviewee) and a plotline. Every interviewee has a *goal* he or she is working toward. In the process, the interviewee is confronting or has confronted some sort of *obstacle*. Usually the story revolves around how your interviewee is looking for or has found an *answer* to this problem. And of course, every struggle like this takes place over *time*—when the goal was first conceived, how the obstacle presented itself, what led to the solution, where the process will be five years from now, and so on.

How does it work? Let's say you have to interview a champion flagpole sitter. Before you go into the interview, you already know his (or her) name, what the record is, and some other preliminary background data—or at least you should. So when you sit down with this flagpole sitter, your mind goes blank. You've forgotten everything you wanted to ask. But that's okay, because you only have to remember the acronym GOAT.

So you start with *goal questions*.

- What are you trying to accomplish?

- What is your purpose for doing this?

- Can you foresee a successful outcome to this situation? What will that look like?

What is a flagpole sitter's goal? To sit up there the longest, of course! But seriously, there has to be a reason behind this. "Tell me," you say casually, "what is your real purpose for doing this?" You may find out that the flagpole sitter has a rare disease, and this is the only way to publicize the need for research. Or, you may simply find that the flagpole sitter likes to do unusual things as an escape from the humdrum of life. Score one for human interest.

What about *obstacle questions*?

- What problems did (or do) you face?

- What stands in your way now?

- Who is your opposition? Why do they disagree with your approach?

What kind of things keep a flagpole sitter up at night? Are there dangers to flagpole sitting? What does one *do* up there all that time? The possible questions are endless (well, not endless, exactly, but you know what I mean).

Your interviewee must have *answers* to these problems.

- How did you handle the crisis?

- Has the new method solved the problem?

- What is your plan for resolving the conflict?

Back to the flagpole sitter. You ask how he handles boredom, how he eats, sleeps, etc. Your story may even include "professional's tips" on flagpole sitting!

Finally comes *time*.

- When did the program begin?

- Whose idea was it? When did you come on board?

- Where do you think you'll be a year from now?

What kind of time questions would you ask a flagpole sitter? "When did you first start flagpole sitting?" comes easily to mind. He may even know something about the history of flagpole sitting in general—how it began, if it ever had a heyday, etc.

There is no reason, of course, to follow the G-O-A-T order in asking questions; as you begin using it, you'll find that answer or time questions may pop into your mind even before you get a chance to talk about goals. In addition, other questions may occur to you that don't even fit the GOAT formula. That's fine, because the purpose of GOAT is to warm up your mental engines, not necessarily to carry you all the way down the road.

GOAT can also surprise you—it may break open an interview and provide you with some unexpected information. I once was interviewing an insurance investigator about a mundane story for the local paper. Just as I was finishing up, I decided to ask a time question—just out of curiosity. "When did you get into insurance investigation?"

That started him into a long discussion of his previous career as a private investigator and concluded with a description of his final case—an as-yet unsolved murder!

Not every interview needs a GOAT, but it's a great comfort when the fear that you won't know what to ask next creeps in. And once you relax, your interviewee will relax too, and everything will go smoother.

Asking the Right Questions

Along with the GOAT method of interviewing, my journalism professor, Dr. Lee Brown, gave his classes a list of the types of questions that elicit meaningful answers and help to clarify vague responses. "Questions that are not thought out, are poorly phrased, or simply irrelevant will produce copy that reflects incompetence," he said. Dr. Brown was not one to mince words.

Here is my version of the list of question types, with examples:

1. Compare and/or contrast: How are the two plans similar? What do you see as the main difference between them?

2. Decision for or against: Do you think it is fair to say that the policy change was a mistake? Why or why not?

3. Application: How might this program work in a larger institution?

4. Classification: What kinds of mistakes do young pastors make?

5. Cause and effect: What do you think caused this loss in attendance? or What seems to be the result of the change in policy?

6. Example or illustration: Can you give me an example of the type of problem you are talking about?

7. Statement of aim: Why do you oppose purchasing the property?

8. Criticism: What weaknesses do you see in your opponent's argument?

9. Inference: From what you know about his background, how will he react in this situation?

10. Discussion: Can you discuss the details surrounding the recent merger?

11. Outline: What are the major parts of the issue?

12. Definition or Explanation: How do you go about defining "obscenity"?

13. Recall: From your research on the issue, what are the most effective solutions?

14. Summary: What were the major points made during the meeting?

15. Observation: What did you notice when you came into the room?

16. Formulating new questions: What questions have occurred to you as you have studied the problem?

Each of these question types will produce certain kinds of information. Which ones you should use, and in what combination, depends on the interview situation. With experience, you will learn the right mix to get the clear, precise answers you need.

Public Research

While private research is excellent for acquiring anecdotal information and analytical information, public research is excellent for preliminary overview information, as well as facts, statistics, etc. upon which to verify and interpret private research—and vice versa. And that's one of the fun things about research: it's often contradictory. So you need to play your sources off one another to judge the value of the information.

Public information may rock a few of your most cherished preconceptions, as well. It can force you to separate the parts of your personal storehouse of information into that which was obtained by actual *observation* (which is more reliable) and what is based on hearsay (which is less reliable). Did you know, for example, that a large percentage of adults—a majority, in fact[1]—believe that "God helps those who help themselves" is in the Bible? A quick review of a good concordance will prove that wrong.

Another very important issue in public research is that you will need to document your sources—in other words, be able to show *where* the information you gathered came from. So make it a habit to write down the author, title, publisher, date of publication, and the page number(s) from which you obtain your information. For a magazine, write down the author, title of the article, name and issue date of the magazine, and the page number. For a website, write down the URL. Avoid using information from a website if possible, because they are often "here today, gone tomorrow." I'll discuss web research in more detail in a minute.

Where to Start with Public Research

Haunt the local library. If you can get a connection with a good college or university library (perhaps through the alumni association), it can be invaluable, but many communities have public libraries with an amazing collection and a comprehensive array of services. Look for one with a good interlibrary loan system, and make friends with the librarians. Tell them you are writing a book, and most librarians will be duly impressed.

Librarians usually get into the business because they love to do research. Give them a research problem and they will take to it like a hound dog to a scent. My first book, *Father to Nobody's Children: The Life of Thomas J. Barnardo*, presented that type of research problem. Barnardo lived in the UK and died in 1905; I had to depend exclusively on previously published material for my sources.

I was able to put the book together by compiling and rewriting information from a half-dozen books that were published about him during his lifetime or shortly thereafter. But *Father to Nobody's Children* would never have become a reality if not for the excellent work of the folks at the Dauphin County (PA) Library System. They tracked down all those old books and had them shipped from libraries halfway across the country. That is why they hold a prominent and well-deserved position in my acknowledgments page.

Be cautious when using Internet research. You can spend too much time to get too little information, much of which may be questionable. The Internet has a wealth of information—but it is also a haven for lies, distortions, and plagiarism. So what does this mean for writers? Simply that you must be careful about the information you use from the Internet. Here are some rules of thumb for judging the quality of the material you receive on the web:

1. Check the web site for authorship. Is it affiliated with a known organization? Does it include a legitimate address, phone number, etc.? Does it include links to other legitimate web sites? Does the authorship imply a definite bias? (Obviously, a Serbian web site will have a different viewpoint than a Bosnian or Croatian site.)

2. What does it look like? Are the graphics sophisticated? Is the text well written, or are there multiple typographical errors and grammatical mistakes? One can assume that when time and money are invested in a site, care will also be taken to get the facts straight.

3. Look for the date of the material. Most legitimate web sites identify when the material was last updated. Without that information, you could be depending on material that is five or more years old—and with many subjects, a lot can change in five years.

4. Is it obviously slanted? Are multiple viewpoints presented, or is all the information one-sided? To give one example, I learned from a web site about Macedonia that Greece has accused the Macedonians of falsifying history and stealing the name "Macedonian." This is a complex issue involving historical and cultural questions that date back to before the time of Christ. The web site appears to present both sides of the argument, so I am more likely to trust it.

5. Don't use a single web site as your only source of information. Check multiple web sites and/or other sources. If your sources contradict each other, look for a majority consensus, or use the rules I've already mentioned to decide which sources are most trustworthy.

These suggestions are not meant to discount the Internet as a source of information; when used carefully, it can be a rich resource. As with everything in this world, however, we need to be "as shrewd as snakes and as innocent as doves" (Matthew 10:16). A little sanctified skepticism never hurts.

Bible Research

Researching the Bible is easily the most important and one of the most abused forms of research. It is crucial that the concepts in your book are the result of a thorough interaction with the Word of God. That is why, in some sense, studying Scripture is both public and private research—it is public in that everyone has access to the Bible, but it is private in that it is one book that researches *you*. More than any other written material, Scripture can actually change your way of thinking as "it judges the thoughts and attitudes of the heart" (Hebrews 4:12).

Too many writers, however, try to *use* Scripture rather than *serve* Scripture. For example, they may decide to write about "joy." After determining what they want to say about the topic, they look up a couple of Bible verses, picking and choosing what will bolster their argument. They treat the Bible like a quote book, creating a theology of sound bites.

Instead, the Christian writer should study to find out what *all* of Scripture has to say about the topic, and in what context. When it comes to the subject of joy, for example, the apostle Paul wrote prolifically about it—even as he was chained to the wall in a rat-infested prison. Puts Christian joy in a completely new light, doesn't it?

Therefore, researching Scripture should be done early in the process, and as it judges the thoughts and attitudes of your heart, it may even drive you back to brainstorming, since you are no longer pooling what you thought you already knew, but getting God's perspective on the subject.

Here are some basic principles for studying a passage:

1. Read the passage yourself first. Don't be tempted to read commentaries about the passage at this stage. After you have read it once, read it again—and again, and again. Read it until you can put its message into your own words.

2. Look for interconnections between words. Are certain words repeated? Who or what is doing the action in the sentences? Who or what is being acted upon?

3. Note what literary form the passage is in. Is it historical narrative, poetry, instruction, etc.? How does this literary form affect the meaning of the passage? (For example, a passage of poetry can often be expected to contain metaphor, hyperbole, and other dramatic literary devices, but a historical passage is usually a straightforward report.)

4. Read the context of the passage as well. Read the preceding and following chapters. *Reread* until you begin to see how the passage in question relates to the rest of the chapter, and/or the rest of the book.

5. Check related texts. Read other Scripture passages that contain the same topics, concepts, or words.

Now you can look at commentaries from other authors, and be able to weigh their statements based on your own in-depth study, rather than simply taking everything they say as true, or slavishly copying their ideas.

Some writers try to impress an editor with their study of Scripture, yet they fall flat. One author, working on a book about how to bring your faith into your workplace, told me in a query letter that he had looked up "all the 419 passages that contain the word *work* in the Bible." My response was as follows:

> We are willing to look at your proposal, but I have one word of caution concerning the concept of your book. Of the 419 passages containing the word *work* in the Bible, I find it doubtful that every one of them refers to one's employment or ministry, per se. On the other hand, there are undoubtedly passages in Scripture that may not use the word *work* but are pertinent to the subject of one's ministry, career, profession, etc. It is important that an author's material grows out of a thorough study of the Word.

The importance of seeing the context of a passage of Scripture came home to me recently when I received a manuscript for a devotional book which included the verse, "A false balance is an abomination to the Lord, but a just weight is his delight" (Proverbs 11:1 KJV). After quoting this verse, the author went on to discuss the importance of maintaining physical, social, and spiritual "balance" in one's life. A closer look at the passage reveals that the word *balance* refers to a grocer's scale, *not* balancing one's daily needs and responsibilities, and the verse is saying that God hates it when a merchant cheats his customers by rigging his scales. No doubt there are passages of Scripture that discuss maintaining proper balance in one's life, but Proverbs 11:1 is not one of them.

What concerned me most about this author (who, by the way, has an impressive string of writing credits) was her reaction to the error I pointed out. "Oh, that's no problem," she responded. "I can find another Bible verse." But that was hardly the point. I didn't want another "proof text"; I wanted evidence that this author had spent serious time in the study of the Scriptures, and that the ideas and concepts expressed in her writing had grown out of her Scripture study. While I don't expect all our authors to be Bible scholars, I do expect them to be students of the Word. If this author had spent more time studying what the Bible says, and less time trying to find support for her ideas in the Bible, she would have had a much more successful proposal.

Dealing with Contradictory Research

It is not unusual to encounter serious contradictions between various sources of research. Analysis of your information involves comparing the discrepancies and attempting to resolve the differences.

For example, let's say I wanted to write a book on youth group events and activities, with a chapter on camping trips. Perhaps I've already done my personal research, and from my personal observation, such trips seemed to be of great value. Perhaps I took my youth group out camping, and everyone grew closer and had a great time.

However, as I begin to do my public research, I may find a real contradiction. What if I look at several books and articles on conducting youth group events, and find that they generally discourage camping? Maybe I will read several authors, and find a recurring theme, which seems to be, "Kids today have no interest in camping."

In desperation, I decide to conduct phone or e-mail interviews with a number of youth group leaders. The response is mixed: some have done camping and love it, some think it is a terrible idea, and still others have never tried it at all.

How do I analyze these findings? I can start by asking myself some tough questions:

- Is it possible my youth group is a fluke? Is there something different about the kids I work with that makes them respond more positively to camping?

- What is the audience for the books and articles I have read? Are the books and articles oriented toward big churches or small churches? Do the authors work with urban, suburban, or rural teens? How old are these articles and books? Is it possible I am on the cutting edge of a new trend?

- How about these youth pastors and leaders I've interviewed—is there any pattern to their responses? Does the success of a youth group camping trip depend on the size of the group, or the area of the country, or the particular culture the church is in?

By playing research results off one another, it is often possible to get to the deeper truth of a subject, and have a more in-depth book.

How to Use Research

How you use research depends on the genre, or kind of book, you're writing. For example:

Devotional: One interesting fact you observe or read about, or someone else told you, could be the basis for an entry in a devotional. Do you remember the situation I mentioned in the brainstorming chapter about my mother feeling like the third verse of a hymn?

Topical book: Spice up the message on a topic with quotes from others, anecdotes from your own experience, or excerpts from a popular book.

How-to: Interviewing several other people who are experienced in the subject of your book will give the topic a much broader and more comprehensive flavor than if you simply write from your own experience.

It is important to notice that public research is often prevalent in nonfiction, while private research (especially personal observation) is often prevalent in fiction. Yet both types of research are critical to both nonfiction and fiction. For example, a single, thirty-year-old female novelist who wants to include a character who is a married male in his sixties would do well to read articles from periodicals such as *Mature Living* and *AARP The Magazine*, and research the demographics on that age group (i.e., public research). And in the same way, if you, the nonfiction author, are writing about temptation, it may be best to begin by asking yourself what *you* have experienced concerning temptation—and interview others, as well.

Now that you are armed with all this research material, you are ready to create the skeleton for your book: the outline. For many writers, the idea of imposing a stiff structure onto what has so far been a fun, creative project is the most depressing thing they can think of. If you are feeling that way, grit your teeth and turn the page. I think you'll be in for a pleasant surprise.

RESEARCH TIP #1:

Photocopy the page(s) of any book or magazine you plan to quote. Later on, you'll be glad you did, because it will allow you to easily verify the endnote information and double-check the wording.

RESEARCH TIP #2:

After you've done some Bible research for your book, run it by your pastor, who should be able to amplify and clarify the work you've done.

RESEARCH TIP #3:

Social media (Facebook, LinkedIn, etc.) can be an easy way to do an informal survey—a little too easy, in fact. So be careful to screen the responses. Some people have an opinion about everything, including things they really know nothing about!

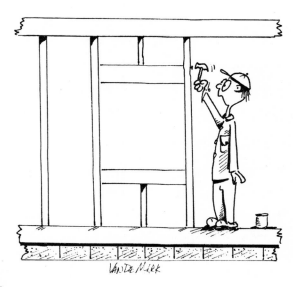

VAN DE MARK

CHAPTER **4**

THE DREADED OUTLINE

> For all my longer works . . . I write chapter outlines so I can have the
> pleasure of departing from them later on.
>
> — Garth Nix

You've developed your ideas and done research to enhance and expand
on them. But they are still in a rather disjointed mess. Now is the time
to organize them into some sort of format, what we usually call an
outline. But for many people, the word *outline* is a terrifying word,
dredging up memories of your fifth-grade English teacher, who was
determined to teach how to do an outline properly—even if neither of
you survived the process!

And you were probably taught to do it all wrong. If your fifth-grade
teacher was like mine (her name was Mrs. McGillicuddy—a dear
soul, and quite long-suffering), you were told that the only right way

to do an outline was neat and tidy, strictly symmetrical, and very standardized. You had your creative fun with brainstorming, and now it was time to get down to business, squeezing all the creativity out of those ideas by forcing them into a regimented structure.

I'm here to tell you that our English teachers were just plain wrong. Much as I loved Mrs. McGillicuddy, she didn't know what she was talking about! The traditional method of outlining—with major points, subpoints, and sub-subpoints—is intrinsically flawed for a number of reasons:

It's structured for a research paper, an academic format that is notoriously boring. And why is it boring? Because it's a writing structure designed for the convenience of the author, not the reader. "Here is my thesis, and now I'm going to prove it by point one, two, and three." Dull, dull, dull! You haven't given the reader a reason to *care* about whether your thesis is true or not! Make sure your outline is *reader-oriented*.

It's artificially symmetrical. Every major point has at least two or more subpoints in a traditional outline, and ideally, each major point has the same number of subpoints. Real life is not that neat and tidy. When you attempt to force your idea into a symmetrical outline, you end up having to create subpoints under your main points that are repetitious or irrelevant. Besides, it encourages a very structured, uncreative thought pattern.

In the academic world, the outline is often considered an end in itself. That's why in school we were taught at an early age to do elaborate and detailed outlines. In fact, in many academic articles—believe it or not—the outline is placed at the *beginning of the paper!* Can you think of anything more appallingly dull?

The academic community may have a different agenda for the outlining process, but for the book author, the purpose is clear and straightforward: The outline lays out a plan for your book—not a detailed, itemized list, but a general idea of what elements will be in each chapter. The outline is not static—it should grow with your project. Which brings me to my next point:

We were warned in school not to outline before brainstorming, and not to research *before* outlining. What bunk! I've never understood the idea of outlining before you research. Talk about a pooling of ignorance! If you don't do some research first, how can you know enough about the subject to outline it? And if you research *after* you outline and discover information that has different emphases than your outline, what do you do? *Scrap the research?*

Actually, brainstorming, researching, and outlining occur *together*—it's a back-and-forth process. Your outline will probably be quite sketchy at first, and will gradually expand as you learn more and mull over the information you've gathered. An outline is a fluid thing, a general "map" of what the book, and more specifically, the individual chapters, are to comprise. As you think more about your book, as you do more research, your outline should grow and develop. So you do all three processes together—in fact, you'll find that you will return to brainstorming, researching, and outlining throughout the process of writing the first draft, and even when doing revisions.

What I am suggesting is that you change your way of looking at an outline. It is *not* a required document (required by *whom*?). It is a tool that you will find useful, no matter what kind of writer you are, no matter how you do your creative work. Think of it as a *writing plan*, a plan you are in control of. When you are heavy into the creative flow of the book, and you suddenly turn a corner and get lost—you find yourself asking, "What was the next point I was going to make?"— you are not without hope. You can just pull out your trusty outli—no, sorry, your "writing plan"—and get your bearings. Your writing plan helps you make sure you put every element into the book that you wanted to.

Your writing plan also helps you keep from wasting time with a tangential idea. If it doesn't fit into the outline, don't put it in. Of course, if a new idea crops up that is obviously central to the topic of your book, but isn't part of your outline, change your outline to include it—nothing is set in stone. And as an evolving document, the outline is going to change quite a bit—at least at first. The more brainstorming and research you do, the more stable the outline will become.

Some students in my writing workshops are dismayed by the whole idea of having a *plan* for writing the book. Too mechanistic, they say; dams up the creative flow. Those who lean toward this way of thinking want to skip outlining and move on to producing a first draft. They tend to view writing the first draft as an act of discovery; they discover what they want to write as they write it. This "learning by doing" method is a perfectly legitimate technique, but the author should see it for what it is—a type of brainstorming, *not* a process for producing a first draft.

"OK," you say. "You've sold me on outlining. But if I don't build a 'writing plan' the way my English teacher taught me, how do I do it?"

Starting Off on the Right Foot

Writing a nonfiction book is a colossal task, and I look with a mixture of awe and amazement upon those prolific authors who are able to quickly produce a publishable manuscript in a matter of months. How do they do it?

For one thing, these authors have done it many times before, and know how to start on the right foot. They save substantial time by avoiding needless digressions into areas that are off-topic, and their clear focus keeps revision and rewriting to a minimum. This clear focus comes from a good outline, which grows out of a three-fold process: create a purpose statement (including the thesis), identify your genre, and establish chapter divisions. Let's take a look at each of these areas.

Create a Purpose Statement and Thesis

The first step taken by experienced authors in creating an outline is to write a *purpose statement*. This is simply putting your book idea in a nutshell—a single sentence or two—then clarifying and refining that statement. A solid, streamlined purpose for the book is couched in a simple, declarative sentence, and then tightened up by removing all words that say *how* they are going to write the book, and including only the parts that say *what* the book is about.

A good, simplified purpose statement does six things for you:

1. It identifies your audience and their "felt need"—the problem, desire, issue, or question they want answered. (It's only a felt need if they *feel* it; in other words, it is a need that they are clearly aware of. You have to speak to your audience where they are.)

2. It moves on to the answer to the problem—the *thesis* of the book. (Often the thesis identifies the audience's "real" need— the need they are probably *not* aware of.)

3. It shows where to start the opening chapter—with an appeal to that felt need which shows empathy with the reader.

4. It shows you where to go with the rest of the first chapter—with an argument for the book's thesis.

5. It implies what the natural outline of the rest of the book should be—an unpacking of the various aspects of the thesis.

6. Finally, it even gives you a hint as to the best title of the book— just look for the most metaphorical, intriguing, or memorable part of the purpose statement.

Can a purpose statement do all that, and still be a single declarative sentence? Yes, if it is done well. Let me demonstrate with a purpose statement written by a student of mine, and my suggested streamlining of that statement.

Here is the student's version (reprinted here with her permission):

> To produce an intriguing, highly readable book assisting adults in communication (comprehending and utilizing the written

and spoken word, i.e., thought) by unlocking the puzzle of how words are built, neatly packaged in an interesting format with a Christian worldview. On a spiritual level, the purpose is for people to understand THE Word at a deeper, more meaningful level, as led by the Holy Spirit.

Wow, that's a mouthful! Notice that so much of this paragraph describes *how* the book will be written ("intriguing, highly readable . . . neatly packaged in an interesting format with a Christian worldview"). Much of the rest is just wordy. The second sentence suggests an additional benefit of the book, but not the primary benefit.

When this extraneous material is removed, what remains is a concise purpose statement: *To help readers communicate more effectively by unlocking the puzzle of how words are built.*

Here's how this sentence fulfills the six benefits of a good purpose statement:

1. The audience and their felt need: people who want to communicate more effectively.

2. The answer or thesis: you can communicate more effectively if you understand how words are "built" (the author is talking about prefixes, suffixes, and word roots).

3. The beginning of the opening chapter: an appeal to the desire to communicate more effectively (possibly by opening with a personal story of an instance when the author did *not* communicate effectively).

4. The remainder of the chapter: an overview of why learning how words are built can help you communicate more effectively.

5.   The outline for the rest of the book: the various aspects of how words are built (suffixes, prefixes, and roots) and specific ways they help in communication.

6.   The title of the book: grows out of the most metaphorical ("unlocking the puzzle"), intriguing, or memorable ("how words are built") part of the statement.

Isn't it interesting how a clear and succinct purpose statement can bring you to a point where the book seems to take shape right before your eyes?

If you're having trouble writing a purpose statement that accomplishes all six of these goals, perhaps you need to come at it from a different angle and consider the *thesis* of the book. The thesis is the answer to the problem, the key to the topic, the point of your argument. It is the heart of a purpose statement, and if you don't have your thesis nailed down, no wonder you can't come up with a purpose statement.

The process for creating and refining a thesis involves getting an objective viewpoint on the subject, a method that goes all the way back to the ancient Latin writers. They had a three-part formula for creating a thesis: *an sit, quid sit,* and *quale sit.* For those who don't speak Latin (including myself), the translation is: *whether it is, what it is,* and *what kind it is.*

This formula may not seem to make much sense at first glance; how does it apply to a thesis for a book? To get a handle on this, let's put these three phrases into the form of questions: *Is it? What is it? What kind is it?* Now let's put these questions into the mouth of an investigator—for example, a detective in a murder investigation.

The homicide detective is called to a "crime" scene. (I put the word *crime* in quotes because, strictly speaking, we don't know whether a crime has taken place yet or not. Remember, we're trying to be objective about this.) The first thing the investigator wants to know is, *Is it?* Did a crime—specifically, a killing—really take place? Maybe the landlord of a boarding house saw a pool of "blood" creeping out from under a tenant's door, so he called the cops. The detective opens the door and finds no body. The tenant left an open can of dark red paint on a table when he left for work, and the cat knocked it over. Whoops! Sorry to bother you, detective. Or maybe the red stuff really is blood, and the tenant is lying in the middle of it, but maybe he's just unconscious. Call the ambulance, and send our detective to the hospital to interview the guy when he wakes up.

But let's say the guy *is* dead. *What is it?* What is the nature of the situation? Was it an accident? Suicide? Murder? Finally, if the detective concludes it's murder, *What kind is it?* What kind of murder is it? Was it premeditated? A murder of passion? (The teary-eyed woman, slumped in the corner with a bloody knife in her hand, is a dead giveaway—unless she's a red herring.) Or maybe it was a stray bullet from a drive-by shooting. There are many possibilities.

Interestingly, once the detective charges someone with murder, the defense attorney uses *an sit*, *quid sit*, and *quale sit* as well:

- Whether it (the defendant) is (guilty): No, he didn't do it—he pleads not guilty.

- What it (the situation) is: OK, he did it, but it's not murder—it was self-defense.

—55—

- What kind (of crime) it is: OK, he did it, but it was not premeditated, so it's manslaughter.

All right, now that you see how it's done, let's play detective and do an objective investigation of your idea:

Whether It Is. Does "it" (your idea) exist? How do we know it does? How can we identify it? In other words, a good way to start boiling down your idea is to seemingly shoot yourself in the foot—question whether it's true at all! As hard as it is to do, you need to look at your main idea and think about who might disagree with it, and why.

Play the devil's advocate—put yourself in the shoes of a critic, and honestly weigh the arguments they might have against your idea. Is there any validity to any of them? (It would be a truly rare case for there to be no validity at all to the opposition's argument; you would be claiming that all those who disagree with you are irrational fools.) You can make a better argument in favor of your position if you have honestly thought through opposing ideas.

Do you remember how I introduced this chapter? I admitted that most of us tend to think of outlines as creativity killers. My thesis of this chapter (yes, an individual chapter should have a thesis, too) is that an outline is a valuable tool, yet I was willing to admit that such a statement might be a hard sell for some people. If I compare my thesis to a tree, the *an sit* step is where I put the weight of reason against the tree to see how strong the roots are.

After asking whether my thesis is true, I then decide that if it *is* true, there must be reasons why. I had better be prepared to articulate those reasons and defend them with convincing arguments, because I have already acknowledged that not everyone agrees with me. The *an sit* step has the potential to bring the element of *controversy* into your thesis—and in this case, controversy is a good thing.

What It Is. How is it defined? How is it different? How is it the same? By defining what your topic is, you get at the *essence* of the thing. Be clear and concrete; this is no place to get metaphoric. Avoid using a form of the same term to define a term ("a poet writes poetry"). And avoid using a negative statement in defining ("a poet is not a prose writer").

What Kind It Is. What categories does it fit in? What are its qualities? This is the step at which you *should* use the negative, and you *should* use metaphors and similes.

This exercise may lead you to wonder if you really know *anything* about the topic of your book. Don't let that discourage you; let it drive you back to further brainstorming and researching.

Identify Your Genre

Once you have created and streamlined a purpose statement and/or thesis for your book, look at what genre it may fall under. Different types of books will have different structures.

Earlier in this chapter I talked about the outline as a map of where you are going with the book or article. (You see why I like to call it a writing plan rather than an outline?) Let me take the map analogy a little further. You don't draw yourself a map every time you go on a trip, do you? Of course not. You use a standard, pre-printed, or electronic map, put together by a professional cartographer.

Did you know there are also standard "maps" for writing projects? No book has a structure that is entirely unique—and you wouldn't want it to be. The chapters and sections should follow a familiar, logical progression, or the reader is apt to get lost and stop reading.

What I am talking about is formula writing, a concept that went out of favor years and years ago. Why did it go out of favor? Most people who oppose formula writing suggest that by using a formula, your writing becomes *formulaic*. It seems like a convincing argument—until you realize that *everything* is written according to some kind of formula. Ironically, those who wrote articles opposing formula writing followed a formula in writing their articles!

Admittedly, following a formula *can* result in formulaic writing, but that's where the writer's creativity comes in. You take the basic formula and put your own unique twist on it. Not only that, but there is not one basic formula, either; the formula varies according to the type (otherwise known as the *genre*) of book:

Biography: Of course, you are telling the story of someone's life. But you have a choice here: you can do it chronologically, from birth to death; or, you can do it topically, covering different aspects of the person's life. In writing a biography of Thomas Barnardo, *Father to Nobody's Children*, I found that it worked best to do a generally chronological structure, but at certain points in the man's life, it was easier to deal with topics. So mine was a hybrid format.

Devotional: Often, a devotional book is structured with daily or weekly sections, each with a standard one-page or two-page format, such as a Scripture reading, commentary on the passage, and a closing prayer. But a devotional book can also be written in a standard chapter format, similar to a Christian living title. And some longer formats in this genre, such as one-year daily devotionals, will often break up the daily routine with special readings at the beginning of each month or the end of the week.

Go to your local Christian bookstore and look over the various devotionals on the shelves. You will find quite a variety of structures within the genre, from short, one-year formats to much longer readings, sometimes the length of a regular chapter book. Many people don't realize it, but *The Purpose-Driven Life* is, for all practical purposes, a forty-day devotional book.

Many novice writers seem to gravitate toward the devotional format. And the attraction is understandable, because the devotional format seems easy: a series of short, self-contained homilies in a standard structure, such as a Scripture quote followed by commentary (the body of the devotional) and a poem or prayer. A devotional book avoids many of the more difficult tasks of the nonfiction writer, such as keeping the reader's attention through lengthy chapters, and interconnecting the chapters to a main theme—or so it seems.

In reality, however, it only *appears* to avoid such difficulties, because a successful devotional book still needs a main theme to unify it, and if each day's reading covers the same general theme, the writer has to work hard to keep the readings from becoming repetitive or from going off the subject. I think that's why I've met so many authors who set out to write a one-year devotional, and stopped at forty, sixty, or ninety days!

Another factor critical to the success of a devotional is its unique slant. Unless you are aiming at a specific audience and are perceived as a knowledgeable person in that audience, there is little chance of getting published—because, frankly, who is interested in some unknown person's thoughts on some Bible passage or topic of faith? But if you address issues of faith related to an area where you can speak with authority—specific career, ministry, problem, etc.—others will want to hear what you have to say.

Christian Living: This is usually a book on a specific topic. (That's a vague statement, isn't it? Most professionals in Christian publishing freely admit that this is a catchall category.) In a Christian living book, the opening chapters usually discuss the *definition* of the topic. Later chapters give *distinctions*, or show what makes the topic distinct from other topics. Other chapters show the *application* of this truth to one's daily life. And at least one final chapter provides a *conclusion*. This is probably the most common formula for a Christian book. Thousands of books use this same basic structure, but there are so many variations on the theme that it's a formula that never grows old.

A variation on this formula is one I like to call the "extended metaphor" structure. The opening chapter begins by introducing the book's thesis couched in a metaphor; often this metaphor is introduced through a compelling and memorable anecdote. A brilliant example of this formula is a book by Gordon MacDonald on reevaluating the focus of life as you reach middle age. It is entitled *Mid-Course Correction*, and uses the metaphor of navigating a ship; a nautical theme is threaded throughout the book.

How-to: A how-to book *identifies the job* to be done or the problem to be solved, *lists the materials or resources* needed to do it, *presents detailed instructions* (which may or may not be step-by-step or as simple as "one-two- three") and as a conclusion, *provides an evaluation or recap* of the job. The second-person imperative ("do this, do that"), while often frowned upon in other types of writing, is perfectly acceptable to use—in fact, nearly impossible to avoid—in this genre.

Some might view this genre as rather unspiritual, relegating the "how-to" format to the shelves of the local hardware store. But I would like to bring to your attention one of the most profound books ever written by A.W. Tozer (hardly a spiritual lightweight), which fits comfortably into this category—*How to Be Filled with the Holy Spirit.*

Current Issue or Exposé: This book begins by *revealing* the problem or issue, then goes into *specifying* where the errors lie, *showing* the results of errors, and finally, *presenting* an alternative. Such a book, especially if it falls into an exposé format, can be highly controversial, so it needs to be well researched and documented (in other words, plan to have numerous endnotes).

Some authors shy away from this genre for fear of becoming contentious, argumentative, polemic—in other words, they don't want to draw a line in the sand. Not everyone is called to such a ministry, though certainly some may be, such as the prophets of the Old Testament. But the issue/exposé genre does not require you to live in the desert and eat locusts and wild honey. A book in this genre need not be written in a strident tone, with warnings of apocalyptic disaster if its counsel is not heeded. If you have noticed a problem or need that seems to be ignored or misunderstood, this genre may be ideal for your book.

Anthology: Do you have editorial skills? Have you ever considered doing a compilation or anthology? This is the art of choosing, organizing, and showcasing the works of other authors. Such books can be very successful and have a significant ministry.

A compilation project involves finding sources for material, copyrights, reimbursing authors, and editorial discernment. But first you need to decide what type of anthology you want to do. Here's a baker's dozen:

1. **A topical book based on a series of sermons or speeches by one person:** This involves editing down transcripts of messages into written form. This is a very common practice; Chuck Swindoll's books, for example, appear to be done this way. Typically each message becomes a chapter, but sometimes it's more complicated than that. Even the best sermons can be less strictly structured than a book chapter. If editing and chapter structure are your thing, here's a project for you.

2. **A devotional based on selections from a single author:** This consists of arranging appropriate excerpts from the works of a well-known, prolific author into a devotional format, adding elements such as Scripture readings and prayers. If you want to compile such a devotional, use a long-dead classic author, whose works are public domain, or you'll have to strike a deal with the author's publisher.

3. **A multi-author devotional:** The driving force of these devotionals is the topic, not the authors, so unknown authors may be used. Even well-known authors may be used, if their publishers are willing to grant permission for a modest fee. One big headache in this kind of project is keeping track of permissions, fees paid to the authors, and other details.

4. **Multi-author first-person stories or chapters, centered on a theme:** This is very similar to the multi-author devotional, but since the text of each author is longer, the editorial work, permissions, and fees can be more complicated.

5. **Modernized version of an old book:** Many classic books have great spiritual messages, but their verbiage and structure are too archaic for modern readers. If you can edit such material to make it more accessible, go for it! Just be sure the book is old enough to be in public domain, or contact the publisher.

6. **Biography based on letters and diaries:** If you write a biography of a deceased person, the only way to let them speak is through their writings. Even if the person is alive, their diaries, journals, and letters can be better than a direct interview. And some biographies are simply edited compilations of letters and journal entries, such as *The Diary of Anne Frank.*

7. **Biography or history compiled and written from older books:** I wrote a biography of Thomas Barnardo, who started orphanages in Victorian London. But I had no access to his letters or journals, and anyone who knew him was long dead. My solution was to read what others had written about him,

then compile and rewrite this public-domain material. The result was the book *Father to Nobody's Children*.

8. **Reformatting a book into devotional segments, with added material:** Edythe Draper divided a book by A.W. Tozer into thirty-one readings and added sidebar material from other authors to create *The Pursuit of God: A 31-day Experience*. Of course, such a project requires the publisher's cooperation.

9. **Quote book:** Short, pithy excerpts from other writers can be fun to compile. If you collect quotes from various authors on one topic, you may not need to pay, or even ask permission, since they are brief. However, if you collect quotes from one author on various topics, you need to get permission for any copyrighted material.

10. **Creative presentation of previously-published material:** Leona Choy took excerpts from classic authors' writings on the Holy Spirit and arranged them with appropriate questions into an "interview" format to create the book *Powerlines*. Perhaps you can come up with a similar creative idea.

11. **Festschrift:** This is a collection of articles by colleagues, former students, etc. in honor of a scholar. If you have contacts in academia, you may be able to do a project like this.

12. **Collection of papers or presentations given at a conference:** This can be a compilation of papers from an academic conference, or written versions of popular conference seminars and workshops. You will need to arrange this with the conference leadership ahead of time.

13. **Collation of articles, or papers:** These are academic papers or popular articles, usually previously published by a particular organization, journal or magazine. Such compilations are often published annually—the "best of" articles or papers from this publication or group. As with a conference, you need to get the cooperation of those in charge. In fact, sometimes an organization will hire someone to do a compilation for them. There's no reason why that person can't be you!

Biography, devotional, Christian living, how-to, issue/exposé, anthology—these are just a few of the genres you may consider. Investigate other possibilities at booksellers' websites, your local Christian bookstore, or the library. There are many formulas or structures, many varieties of each general category, and many examples of hybrid formats, where two different genres have been merged into one book. After you learn what you are looking for, however, they can be easy to spot.

Here's an exercise for you: get three magazine articles (or if you're ambitious, three books) and study each of them for the basic outline or formula used. How is the topic introduced? How is it built? How does it conclude? And that leads to the most basic of all formulas: every book, and every chapter within a book, has a beginning, a middle, and an end.

Every writer follows some kind of structure or formula when writing a book. If you do it consciously rather than subconsciously, you'll end up with a better result.

Establish Chapter Divisions

Sort through your brainstorming notes and your research to find the major points to your book idea, and then assign them a particular order. After more brainstorming and research, you may add other major points until your list of chapters seems complete. (You can tell the list of chapters is complete when your research and ideas start producing subpoints under the chapters rather than entirely new aspects that are not covered by any particular chapter.)

How many chapters should a book have? The basic skeleton of any nonfiction book is somewhat standardized, and most books have eight to fourteen chapters. But just as a football team has a wide field between the sidelines in which to run plays, you have a great amount of liberty within the general structure of a book. In fact, unlike a football team, your boundaries are flexible; it is not necessarily wrong, for example, to have fewer than eight chapters, or more than fourteen. The book with more than fourteen, however, may have a thesis too big for a single book, or it may have very short chapters that need to be merged. A book with fewer than eight chapters may be trying to say too much in each chapter, or the thesis may be more appropriate for an article than a book. There seems to be a natural limitation— and yet, it's a limitation that is ignored frequently. We could easily go to any bookstore and find dozens of successful titles that violate the eight-to-fourteen chapter "rule." I hesitate to call it a rule. Let's just say that an outline should not stifle your creativity.

And as you determine your chapters, you will find that your choice of genre can help you in the outlining process. If you can't figure out a logical order for the chapters, find a book in the same genre and look at how the author of that book ordered the chapters. It may help you find the right logical structure for your book.

After identifying your chapters, do some more brainstorming and research, and then you can start to develop an outline of each chapter, identifying the major points you want to make within the chapter, and maybe even some specific illustrations, quotes, and anecdotes you plan to include. But don't worry if it seems incomplete or awkward—remember, it's a *writing plan*, not an exact formula.

As you begin the later steps of preparing the proposal, writing the rough draft and taking the manuscript through revision, you'll be carrying this outline along with you, letting it guide you, and sometimes revising it as you see fit. It's not set in stone.

You may decide that one of your chapters really has two major ideas, each so important that you need to expand it into two separate chapters. Or you may conclude that two chapters are so interrelated that they can be merged. Remember, your English teacher isn't here, so you can do whatever you want with the outline. (I especially like Garth Nix's comment at the beginning of this chapter.)

But if you've done your job well, I think you'll find that the outline gradually develops into a comfortable pattern, one that is clear, logical, and progressive. It starts at a point of common ground with the reader and takes them step-by-step to an inevitable conclusion.

What does a real-life outline look like? By now you probably see that it can look like anything you want, as long as it helps you plan out your chapters. Let me give you the outline of a chapter for a book I am working on called *A Question of Balance*:

CHAPTER FIVE: Walking the Narrow Path

Opening: Anecdote/illustration? [I haven't found one yet]

Definition: Narrow path between extremes.

Distinctions: What "Narrow Path" is *not*:

1. Not legalistic

2. Not life of a hermit (story of Howard Hughes)

3. Not limiting or stifling (football sidelines analogy)

Application: How this is lived out:

— examples

— features

— benefits

Conclusion: Get a good example of someone who epitomizes this. End with a transition into Chapter Six.

Can you see that I am still at a rough stage in this outline? Eventually, I will get more specific in much of the chapter. The "application," especially, is sketchy. But it will work itself out.

Getting even a rough outline/writing plan developed should really get the creative juices flowing, and spur you on to the next step. But there is a surprise waiting for you in the next chapter, because the "next step" is not what you think.

OUTLINING TIP #1:

If you're really stuck on how to outline your book, take a published book that you admire (preferably in the same genre) and analyze how it is structured. That can often help you see your own book in a new light.

OUTLINING TIP #2:

Are you unsure of what genre (category) your book fits into? You may get some insight from someone who works in a bookstore or library. Sharing your idea with a person who is familiar with different types of books can result in invaluable feedback.

OUTLINING TIP #3:

Your outline doesn't have to look like anyone else's outline. As long as it works for you, it makes no difference if it is complete gibberish to everyone else.

5

BOOK PROPOSALS: THE FRONT-END METHOD

Nine out of ten nonfiction books are contracted from a book proposal, not a full-length manuscript.

— Terry Whalin

Brainstorming, researching, outlining—surely the next step is writing the rough draft! The answer is no, and to explain why, I need to tell you about a crucial document you are about to create. This document is designed to convince a sometimes skeptical publisher to invest the company's limited funds in your writing project. It is called a book proposal.

Of the multitudes of book proposals that come across my desk, I think it would be generous to say that one in ten is complete and well-prepared. I am not being tough, just honest.

And it makes me ask the question—why? There are plenty of articles and books that tell the basic components of a book proposal. Let me stop here and briefly list them. We will discuss them in more detail later.

1. Cover Letter

2. Premise Statement

3. Audience/Market

4. Competitive Titles

5. Author Information

6. Chapter-by-Chapter Synopsis

7. Sample Chapters

The required information may vary a bit among publishers, but these are the basic parts of a proposal. And yet regularly I get proposals–even from experienced authors—that are missing pieces. Otherwise they are well-done, but because they lack crucial information, I am hampered in making a decision.

So, why? Why don't authors provide a complete proposal?

Part of it is surely that authors do not realize how important the proposal is. The author is essentially presenting a sales pitch to the acquisitions editor. The proposal has to be complete, because the editor has to use it to sell the book to the acquisitions team, who sells it to the publishing committee, who will make the final decision. By writing a complete proposal, you give an editor the ammunition he needs to pitch your book to his or her company. Do most authors understand the importance of a clear and complete proposal? I suspect not.

But there's another, bigger reason why authors don't provide complete proposals. It's because they're going about it backwards. First, they write the book, then they prepare the proposal. On the surface it seems to make sense: before you can sell the book to a publisher, you have to write it first, right? It sounds logical, but it's a process that's doomed to failure.

I want to tell you about what I call the front-end method of writing a proposal. Simply put, it's the idea of doing the proposal at the front end of the book project—*before* the book is written, sometimes even before the outline seems fully developed. There are two reasons to do this.

First, it capitalizes on your energy level. Occasionally, I will get a full book manuscript from someone with nothing but a cover letter that says something like, "Here's my book—either publish it or throw it out; I'm sick of looking at it!" I can appreciate the feeling. The author has been through a grueling process—writing a book is equivalent to giving birth, except that the labor pains last all nine months! (For some reason, mothers don't seem to like that joke.) Writing a book is hard; it's exhausting. Then you have to turn around and sell it to an editor. Why torture yourself? Write the proposal early in the process, when the idea is fresh and your creativity is really hopping.

But you want to write that first draft, don't you? I'll bet you're afraid you might use up all your energy on the proposal and have nothing left for the book. But there's nothing to worry about on that score—in fact, it leads into the second reason for doing the proposal first:

It streamlines the writing process. The discipline of gathering the information and putting together the skeleton of your book on paper serves to *focus your ideas*, helps you identify places that need to be researched further, and smooths out potential snags in the project. Your proposal becomes a "to-do" list, much as your outline does.

Before I wrote my first book, I tried to research a systematic method for doing it. You know what? There's not much out there in step-by-step methods for writing a nonfiction book. (Remember the quote I started with in the first chapter: "There are three rules for writing a book—unfortunately, no one knows what they are!") But when you prepare a good proposal, you can use it as a guideline for completing the project. It helps everything fall into manageable pieces, and keeps your writing on track.

Ah, but there's the rub! Putting together the proposal may seem harder to do than writing the book. But you have to look at it this way: your work on the proposal is *clearing the path* to writing the book. It's not a waste of time. With that in mind, you can attack the job of the book proposal with much more optimism.

Now that we have our heads on straight, let's look at the elements of a complete proposal in more detail.

Cover Letter

The last thing you should write is the cover letter, which is like an abbreviated version of the entire proposal. Briefly, it consists of three paragraphs: the first is a hook—present the problem, issue, topic in an interesting way; the second is an abbreviated premise statement (which we'll talk about later) and one or two of the strongest points from the rest of your proposal; the third is details—length, how soon it can be completed, etc. Finally, conclude your letter with a brief statement such as, "I look forward to hearing from you." One exception to this format: if you are sending the proposal to an editor who requested it, begin the letter by reminding the editor of that fact: "It was good to meet you at the So-and-So Christian Writers' Conference. Here is the proposal you asked for."

Premise Statement

What is the book about? Think "thesis." Think *an sit, quid sit, quale sit*—whether it is, what it is, what kind it is. Think Problem/Solution. Here is a portion of the premise to a book proposal I received a few years ago:

> Behind the long-standing desire to write something meaningful and maybe even beautiful has been my own need to be real. In these rapid, millennial times—times in which so many of us experience all too often a kind of driven unreality—I frequently have found myself at day's end wondering if my days will endure; I frequently have found myself too tired to care much about anything. And being too tired to care bothers me, compels me to be real, constrains me at least to want to be honest, and leads me to write, not just for myself, but also for others. The concept for the book was spawned out of my own yearning to be real.

What's wrong with this? Has the author told us what the book is about? No. Have we learned *anything* that would interest an editor? No!

Here's the premise statement from the proposal for my book, T*eaching with All Your Heart*:

> Many Sunday school teachers are frustrated with standardized curriculum—not as much with the content as with the format. How can they cover all the steps in the lesson? If class time runs short, what do they cut out? How can they infuse creative ideas into a standardized lesson? *Teaching with All Your Heart* encourages the teacher to take control of the structure and direction of the lesson, and not be intimidated by the curriculum. In an upbeat, non-academic style, this book counsels teachers to use the standardized lesson plan as a guideline rather than a strict checklist. Through a series of simple organizational and memorization techniques, *Teaching with All Your Heart* explains how to present a lesson without repeatedly referring to notes or the manual. This approach allows a teacher to bring a spontaneity and excitement to the lesson that is otherwise difficult to achieve.

Do you know what the book is about?

Audience/Market

For whom are you writing this book? More to the point, who would be willing to pay money to buy this book? Publishers want to know the answers to these questions—and "everyone" is not the answer they are looking for. For one thing, we all know it's just not true that "everyone will want to read this book." (There are some people who would rather lose a limb than read a book.) But even if your book is so compelling that most people would be willing to pick it up, it is critical to identify specific aspects of your book that would appeal to specific groups of people.

Most authors are so close to their book it's hard to look at it objectively, but that is what you have to do to successfully identify your audience. This will help you in the end, however, because it's easier to write to an identified audience than some vague, faceless crowd out there.

Sometimes research and statistical information help, but I've seen many an author lose credibility by quoting some generalized statistic and implying that everyone in that statistical group would buy the book: "This book is for married people. Did you know there are ____ million married people in the United States?" However, if you were writing a book on Christian financial counseling for married couples, you might include a statistic on how often Christian counselors find finances to be the root of marital problems.

Comparative Titles

Take a trip to the Christian bookstore and browse the racks, or take a stroll down "Amazon.com lane." Find three or four current books that are in some way similar to yours and explain why yours is different. It is possible (but rare) that you will find one or more major books that cover exactly the same subject with exactly the same slant. If that were to happen, it would be time to rethink your idea—in other words, go back to brainstorming, researching, outlining!

It is quite unlikely, however, that you will find an exact duplicate of your idea in an already published book—unless your idea is so generic that it sounds like *every other book* on that same subject. If that's your problem, you haven't thought through your unique slant on the subject, and guess what the solution is? That's right—back to brainstorming, researching, outlining!

The irony of all this is that the comparative titles section should not only show how your book *differs* from other books on the market, but also how it is *similar* to others—though, of course, it is not without its own unique slant. The comparative titles section shows where your book fits within the marketplace, as well as what genre it falls under. When you place it alongside other similar titles, your book can really come into focus and establish its niche in the market.

But if you are going to stubbornly insist (as so many authors do) that "there really is no other book like it," those who read your proposal will have a hard time picturing your book in their minds. Your book remains a vague, amorphous thing, and you, the author, will begin to look foolish.

Now that we have the Internet, there are entirely new possibilities for making yourself look foolish. I now frequently receive a report like this in a proposal: "Amazon.com lists 347 books on this subject; 129 are by Christian publishers. I think mine is different because . . ." Oh, *really*? Have you read all 129 of these books? This kind of comparative titles section can actually become an argument *against* publishing your book—and you certainly don't want to convey *that* message!

The best way to bring your book into focus in this section is to compare your book to a limited, representative sample of three or four titles. One of these titles could be a bestseller by a well-known author, but don't use *only* big-selling books. Otherwise the editor is going to question whether you expect to be able to compete with compete with Beth Moore or Max Lucado.

When I prepare the comparative titles section of a proposal, I choose books that are deliberately different than mine (though in the same genre), in order that I might use them to emphasize the features of my book that make it stand out from the rest of the pack.

For example, in the proposal for my book on Sunday school teaching, I identified just three titles. One had many of the same concepts as mine, but pushed the curriculum of one particular publisher; I noted that my methods would work with any curriculum. One taught some basic concepts, but did not emphasize preparation and presentation the way mine did. And the third was a collection of lesson ideas, but did not show the teacher how to prepare those lessons and make them their own—as mine did. From these three books I was able to flesh out the distinctive features of my manuscript, bringing it into clear focus for the editor.

An alternative method for doing the comparative titles section is a general survey of the particular niche in the market for which you are aiming. This can be a risky method, because you are essentially describing the landscape of the book market to a book professional— someone who lives there every day. However, if you have done the kind of research you ought to be doing to write the book, you've probably already become a minor expert in the particular niche you are aiming at. You have probably even read some of the books in that niche.

In my proposal for this book, I realized that I *had* to present myself as an expert in the publishing niche I was aiming for, because the nature of the topic demanded it (the book is *about* Christian writing and publishing, after all!). While I was careful to avoid saying "there's no other book like it," I was able to establish that the top one hundred books in a search for "Christian writing" on Amazon.com revealed not a single title on writing a Christian nonfiction book.

I noted that the general books on Christian writing in the top one hundred contained portions of what I teach in this book (this proved that I was tapping into a common need). However, not one covered the process of writing a nonfiction book comprehensively—or, as I put it in the book's title, from "concept to contract." Score one for uniqueness! (You may have noticed that "tapping into a *common* need with a *unique* slant" harkens back to the "uniqueness/sameness" concept I talked about in the chapter on brainstorming.)

Author Information

The purpose of this section is two-fold: 1) to establish your qualifications or credentials for writing this book, and 2) to highlight potential marketing contacts you might have.

Most authors become stuck on this. But dig deep into your life for credentials. What is your ministry in your local fellowship? Do you belong to any organizations? What makes you different from the next person in the pew? One author I worked with did not have major credentials for her book on teaching spiritual disciplines to children—except that she had raised three children and twenty-five foster children!

Also dig deep for your contacts and opportunities to market the book. Do you have a web site? Do you speak to any groups during the year? Are you *available* to speak? Do you know anyone of influence who might help you promote the book? Brainstorm this with close friends who know you well.

The publisher I work for sometimes asks authors to fill out an information sheet to help prime their pump, so to speak. This form asks for information on family, education, denominational affiliation(s), other published books or articles, editorial or publishing connections, and affiliations, awards, or achievements in business, military, professional, and community fields. The form even includes room to cover hobbies, interests, special skills, unusual experiences, and "other illuminating personal insights." Space is provided as well for the author's personal testimony and spiritual journey.

Responses to these sorts of questions may spark some ideas in the minds of the marketing department. If you can do all this in one-half to one page, that would be just great. Some authors also include a résumé with their proposal. That is not necessary, unless your professional experience and your résumé are exceptional, and in some way related to the topic of your book.

Chapter-by-Chapter Synopsis

Pull out the outline you've created and produce a short paragraph summarizing each chapter. Short means two or three sentences—almost like a premise statement for each chapter. Be clear! But also keep them guessing. Here's the synopsis from one chapter of my book on teaching:

Chapter 6: The Words of Your Mouth

Following the example of Jesus Christ (undeniably the world's greatest teacher), the ancient but still effective practice of *asking questions* is described here, along with other techniques of oral presentation. This chapter draws heavily on the Gospels to find the secrets behind creating provocative discussion questions, using effective transitional statements, and answering students' questions.

Notice how I include just enough information to get you curious?

Sample Chapters

I know, I know, I told you that you're supposed to prepare the proposal even before you write the first draft. Now I'm saying that you should have two or three chapters in final form to include in the proposal. Am I contradicting myself? No, not really; this is simply the point in the writing process where the steps begin to overlap each other.

You should prepare a draft version of the proposal (minus the sample chapters, of course) before writing the first draft. But while you write the first draft, and later, as you take it through the revision stage, you can be continually revising the proposal, honing it into final form. That way, you can be sure your proposal accurately reflects the book. (It's a lot easier to accurately describe the book when it's written and not all in your head.) Writing a draft of the proposal before you start writing the manuscript is very helpful, however, because early drafts of the proposal can give you good feedback for writing the manuscript. Show the draft proposal to several people and listen carefully to their feedback; they will raise questions you need to answer and bring up objections you need to address about your book idea. It's like giving your book idea a test drive.

The feedback you receive is valuable information, and you want it before you've written the book. It's easier to rewrite the proposal than the entire manuscript. So get plenty of feedback before beginning the first draft. But once you get some good feedback, don't hesitate to start on that first draft. The proposal does not have to be in final form before you start putting words down on the page.

I suspect, however, that you might already have a couple of chapters half-written, and they may even be done by the time you finish even the draft of your proposal. Caught you red-handed, didn't I?

But don't be embarrassed; I know how writers think and work. All that brainstorming, researching, outlining, and preparing of the proposal will get you to a point that you are itching to write something—and this kind of temptation is one you can give in to with a clear conscience.

Let me assure you that the eight steps in writing a book—brainstorming, researching, outlining, preparing the proposal, writing a rough draft, revising, finalizing the manuscript, and marketing—are only marginally chronological. You are free to do them in any order you wish—or simultaneously, if you like. The order in which I have placed them is a general guideline. If you looked over the shoulders of experienced authors, you might find them doing the first draft of one chapter, while revising another, and perhaps still in the outlining stage of a third. Meanwhile, they might have their proposal already completed—with sample chapters, of course—and making the rounds of the various publishing houses.

One word of warning, however: when you include sample chapters with your proposal (and most publishers insist on sample chapters, by the way), they had better be very well written. Remember, this is your opportunity to show the editor that you can write. The sample chapter(s) you send must be well polished—don't send a first draft. Ideally, you should include the introduction and/or the first chapter; a chapter from the middle of the book (with a theme built on the foundation of previous chapters) may be confusing and leave a bad impression.

Test-Driving Your Book Proposal

But back to the draft of the book proposal. You don't want to try to use this rough version to pitch to a publisher just yet. You should get some feedback on it first. To whom should you send the draft proposal? Here are some ideas:

- *Give it to a couple of people who would fit the description of your audience.* (If you can't find two people who fit the description, why are you writing this book? Perhaps you will need to rethink your idea, broadening its scope to appeal to more people, and then rewrite the "Audience" section.)

- *Give it to a couple of people who might be considered "experts" in the field.* By that I don't necessarily mean professionals with advanced degrees in the subject (though that's not a bad idea). An expert on the subject could be anyone with knowledge, experience, or skill.

A draft proposal on the subject of evangelism might be given to a friend of yours who is a real soul winner. A proposal for a Bible study could be given to a Bible study leader. Can you think of someone who probably could have written your book? That's a perfect choice.

- *Give it to some other writers and editors.* If you don't belong to a writers' critique group, consider starting one—and then show them your draft proposal. If you don't know any editors, consider attending a writers' conference. This can be the ideal place to give your proposal a trial run.

Ask for and expect honest criticism and suggestions for additional material. Take it all with a grain of salt; weigh the suggestions carefully; consider the source. For example, if you give it to your favorite college professor who then tells you it's too "popular" or not academic enough, remember that this poor soul spends hours poring over research papers and dissertations—and may even enjoy doing so. If a person who barely passed English 101 tries to give you tips on grammar, smile and nod patiently. But if an editor questions your grammar, you probably want to listen!

When I sent the draft proposal of my Sunday school teaching book around to editors at writers' conferences, I discovered an interesting phenomenon: publishers of curriculum said they didn't publish books, and publishers of books said they didn't publish books on teaching, because they didn't publish curriculum. Sounds like a Catch-22, doesn't it? But I realized I needed to approach a larger publisher, one that published books *and* curriculum. The draft helped me find the right market so I wasn't wasting my time.

I also learned in this feedback that my draft proposal was unnecessarily critical of curriculum publishers—the very publishing houses I was trying to sell my book to! I found that a slight rewording in the proposal (which was later reflected in the text of the book) was all that was needed to keep those publishers' feathers unruffled.

Mistakes to Avoid in Preparing a Proposal

Ken Petersen of Random House Publishers made a great presentation at a conference for editors several years ago. Ken pointed out nine mistakes that *editors* make when they present proposals to a publishing committee. These possible mistakes certainly apply just as well to authors in preparing a proposal. Here they are:

1. *Ambiguity:* Be clear when it comes to selling an idea. Ask others to look at your proposal with a ruthless eye. When they identify something that is unclear, thank them profusely!

2. *The Forest for the Trees:* Be thorough with every element of your presentation. It is easy to become excited about one section or aspect of the proposal and let all other parts of it slide.

3. *Overselling:* Be passionate about your book idea, but also be realistic. Don't make extravagant claims, such as "This book will revolutionize the church of the twenty-first century!" Try for a more qualified claim, applied to an individual: "I believe there is new hope for any discouraged Christian who faithfully applies the principles of this book."

4. ***Underselling:*** Blow your own horn. You have to get people enthused. What got you so enthused about the topic that you decided to write a book? Show us your *passion* for the topic.

5. ***Selling Editorial Policy, Not a Manuscript:*** Find out who publishes books like yours, and send your proposal to them. Don't send it to a publisher who never publishes your kind of book. "Your guidelines say you never publish books on this topic, but I just know you'll change your mind, as well as your company's editorial policy, once you see *my* manuscript!" Editors don't have that kind of power or influence. (And not following guidelines is a sign of an amateur writer.)

6. ***Lack of Preparation:*** Don't slap together a proposal. It needs to be a reasoned, carefully executed presentation. Take time to write it clearly and thoroughly.

7. ***Premature Presentation:*** Develop your idea fully before you try to get someone else to invest in it. (And if your idea is not fully developed, you know what that means—more brainstorming, research and outlining!)

8. ***Not Oriented to the Reader:*** Speak to what readers want—their "felt needs," for lack of a better term. Authors frequently say, "Christians *need* to read this book," but the book won't sell unless buyers *know* they need to read it. Does your book meet a need that Christians can *see* that they have? You can't make them buy it and read it.

9. ***Focusing on Features, Not Benefits:*** Proposals often emphasize things like a glossary, or discussion questions at the end of each

chapter. All these are fine to mention, but remember that the concept for the book has to carry the day. How does this book *benefit* the reader?

As you can see, Ken really took us editors to the woodshed. (I have to admit it, but I have made every one of these mistakes myself, at one time or another.) I'm just passing along his friendly admonition.

Get that Proposal Done Early

I always advise authors to prepare a proposal early in the process. It is not unusual to have the proposal completed before you start writing the book. If so, don't be shy about sending a proposal without any chapters to an editor; the feedback you receive can be invaluable in preparation of your manuscript.

Besides, a publisher may send you a contract solely based on your proposal. Having a contract, and an editor breathing down your neck to meet a deadline, is an amazing motivator for an author. (I am experiencing that motivation right now!)

You never can tell—you may even have the pleasant problem that confronted Laura Hillenbrand, author of *Seabiscuit*. In August of 1998, she prepared a proposal for her book on the famous racehorse, and her agent sent it around to a few publishers. Within hours, a bidding war had begun on the as-yet unwritten manuscript, and she signed with Random House before a week had passed. But the best was yet to come. She wrote:

> The next morning, I got a call from a famous movie producer who said he wanted to buy the rights to my book. I have no idea how he

got my number, as I was dog sitting in Maryland. I was starstruck and completely confused; making a film of this story hadn't even occurred to me, and *I hadn't written a single line of the book yet.* I had no idea how this man knew anything about my book proposal.[1]

Laura Hillenbrand had a pleasant problem, don't you think? And if you prepare your proposal well, you may be in the same situation, with a publisher, maybe even a movie producer (we can dream, can't we?), waiting to see this wonderful book—which is yet to be written. How do you bring this rabbit out of your hat? Read on, my friend.

PROPOSAL TIP #1:

Let's face it: writing a proposal is hard to do. You are putting your book idea (which up until now has been a private little dream) on a public stage for the world to see. Get yourself past the embarrassment of public exposure and you're halfway home.

PROPOSAL TIP #2:

Looking for books to include in your comparative titles section? Go to your local bookstore and ask what titles they would recommend on the topic of your book.

PROPOSAL TIP #3:

Ask a trusted friend to read your proposal, and then describe the book. Does your proposal produce a clear picture of the book in his or her mind?

CHAPTER **6**

THE FIRST DRAFT: BEGIN AT THE BEGINNING

The pages are still blank, but there is a miraculous feeling of the words being there, written in invisible ink and clamoring to become visible

— Vladimir Nabakov

There is one point in the writing process that never fails to make me feel like a total amateur, as if I don't know anything about writing. That is when I sit down to write the first draft of a book. The overwhelming size of the project puts me at a loss as to where to begin.

Writing that first draft may seem daunting—and it is! But the solution is to have a battle strategy used by some of the greatest military minds of history: divide and conquer. The best way to attack a big job is to break it down into smaller steps. So with a good, flexible outline and notes of my research at hand, I start cutting this scary giant into smaller, not-so-scary pieces. Here's my secret: I begin by working on one chapter at a time.

Right about now you're probably thinking, *Dave, you're being ridiculously obvious again*, but there's more insight to that advice than you may think. I often find that my writing momentum is stalled by the unconscious habit of trying to write about everything at once. That "everything at once" mentality can even disguise itself as creative momentum, so that I have a flurry of words—only to discover that I've produced three or four pages of slop, containing everything I wanted to say in the whole book (albeit disjointed, disorganized, and dismembered), and I feel like I have nothing more to say.

If I have prepared a good outline, however, those manic, "everything at once" episodes can be avoided. Each chapter should focus on one main idea. As I concentrate on presenting one idea at a time, I can ignore that little voice in the back of my mind that's screaming, *But what about this, and what about that, and don't forget the other thing!* My job becomes easier—and my writing should be more readable.

Even then, the job may seem too big, but thankfully, a book chapter can be cut down into still smaller elements. Write the individual elements one at a time, and then merge them together. A typical book chapter consists of the following pieces:

1. **The Lead Paragraph.** An effective lead will draw the readers in and keep them reading. Introduce the topic in a way that connects with the readers, sparks their curiosity, and promises them something. Just make sure you don't promise them something you can't deliver in the rest of the chapter.

2. **Main Points.** This is straight expository writing—just tell it like it is. Much of this content can be pulled directly off your

outline. If necessary, also include sub-points. If you are stuck as to what to say, fall back on that exercise from ancient Greek rhetoric that I mentioned in a previous chapter: *whether it is, what it is, what kind it is.* "Whether it is" means you ask yourself if "it" (your main point) exists, how do you know it does and how can you identify it. "What it is" means you try to define your main point—try to nail down what it is you are really talking about. And "what kind it is" means you try to identify the distinguishing qualities of your main point, as well as what category it falls under. This exercise can usually get the juices flowing so you can get back on track and say what you want to say.

3. **"Helper" Material.** Each main point needs something to help the reader understand it and remember it. It may be a phrase, a sentence, or several paragraphs; it may be a simile, metaphor, analogy, or anecdote. Regardless, it carries the reader from what they know to what they do not know—a tried-and-true principle of teaching. The "whether it is, what it is, what kind it is" exercise can often spark ideas for "helper" material.

4. **Transitions.** Between each main point, there should be transitional statements that introduce the next main point and show its relationship to the previous one. It is critical to put time into this, because a lack of transitions (not to mention awkward or trite transitions) is one of the most common errors in writing, and one of the main reasons that editors reject a submission.

5. **Conclusion.** Finally, wrap up what you have to say, leaving the reader with something to think about, or with a memorable word picture that anchors the main point of the article or chapter in their brain. This is what editors often refer to as the "take-away" factor. In a book chapter, the conclusion can frequently be used to give a hint of what is to come. This should spark the readers' curiosity and hook them into going on to the next chapter.

The Opening Chapter

Earlier in this book, we talked about how a solid *statement of purpose* for a nonfiction book helps you know where you are going in writing your book. Let's look now at the *opening chapter* of a book, and how it can set the pace for the remaining chapters as well as avoiding the mistakes that inevitably lead to rewriting and revision.

I am assuming that the outline (your *writing plan*) for your book is detailed enough that you have a plan for each chapter as well. Remember, you don't have to do all the steps in chronological order, and you can do more than one at once. However, by the time you start preparing a serious draft of your book, you ought to have done enough outlining to know about how many chapters it will have and what those chapters will contain.

How much detail you put into each chapter's outline is up to you, but my suggestion is to put in a little more detail than you may be comfortable with, knowing that you are free to depart from it if necessary. It's a *map* of the book that helps you keep from repeating information or introducing new information too soon. Instead of going off on rabbit trails, you can say to yourself, *I don't have to get into that issue right now, since I'm covering it thoroughly in another chapter.* But you can only tell yourself that if you've *mapped out* the book in advance. Remember those great words of wisdom: "If you don't know where you're going, you'll probably end up somewhere else."

Your outline probably calls for the book to begin with a preface or introduction, right? I hope not. Prefaces and introductions are largely a waste of time, because most readers never read them. Editors usually blame this on the fast pace of society—everyone sees an introduction as frivolous outer wrapping; readers want to get right to the main point of the material. While there is some truth to that, I think the real culprits in the demise of the introduction are generations of *authors*, who have cluttered their books with dry, mindless introductions that usually begin, "I first knew I wanted to be a writer when I was seven years old." Wow, great stuff. Save it for your memoirs.

I know just what you're going to say: "Well, the introduction in *my* book isn't like that." Of course it's not. Your introduction really *introduces*; it focuses the reader on the problem, issue, or topic of the book. Great! That's just what it should do. An introduction should be so crucial that the reader *must* read it to be on the same page with the author (pardon the pun). That's why I suggest you give this wonderful introduction of yours a special name. Call it "Chapter One."

A nonfiction book, and especially a *Christian* nonfiction book, should solve a dilemma, bring awareness and perspective to an issue, tell the story of someone or something, teach how to do something, provide information, or inspire the reader to greatness. Of course, it probably should do many of these things and more, but its main thrust (based on its statement of purpose) is one single objective. The opening chapter has to tell the reader what that objective is—what the whole book is about—without revealing so many details that the reader thinks there's no need to read further. You don't exactly let the cat out of the bag; you just let the reader see its right paw and whiskers.

What I'm talking about is the use of foreshadowing. If you think that foreshadowing sounds suspiciously like a fiction technique, you're exactly right. In fiction, it is a hint that a twist in the plot, a new character, or something else is coming. For example, you might write in a novel, "Sally was not prepared to tell her friends about what happened last summer." If "what happened last summer" has not yet been mentioned at that point in the novel, the reader starts to wonder what exactly *did* happen, and why Sally is so reluctant to tell her friends. The reader is spurred on by curiosity, knowing that Sally's secret will be revealed eventually. (It had better be, or the editor will surely strike out that sentence about "what happened last summer"!)

Did you know you can do the same in nonfiction? And you don't even have to be that subtle. In my book on Sunday school teaching, I outlined the steps I take in preparing to teach a lesson, then the remaining chapters were each devoted to a different step in the process. (Come to think of it, that's what I do in this book, too!) That's a good way (though not the only way) to write the first chapter: you give your reader an outline of what the rest of the book will cover. But don't let it read like an outline. It has to be interesting.

How to Write When You Really Don't Want To

I have never met a writer who wasn't stalled at some point in writing a first draft. So now seems as good a time as any to discuss that ominous enemy of every author: writer's block.

A few years ago, when I was a freelance editor, I had the opportunity to help a novelist get unstuck and complete his first draft. I looked over what he'd written, made a few observations and suggestions, and that was all he needed. He went on to finish—and publish—the novel. (Frankly, I'm not exactly sure what I said or did to get him unstuck, but I suppose the best kind of advice is subtle.)

It got me thinking about this strange phenomenon we call "writer's block" and the motivation (or to be more accurate, the lack of motivation) behind it. After studying my own and other writers' frustrations, I've concluded that usually we don't write because we really don't want to.

Now before you start throwing bricks in my general direction, think about it. Wouldn't the best way to describe writer's block be that part of you wants to write and part of you doesn't? What could be more frustrating than arguing with yourself? Either way you lose.

As long as we are psychoanalyzing ourselves, let's consider some of the reasons why that other part of you doesn't want to write:

1. **You want it to be perfect.** This is your inner perfectionist saying, "Why do more work than you have to? If you're going to write this, do it right the first time. First drafts, revisions, etc. are wasted energy." But deep down you also know that

you *can't* write it perfectly the first time, so you freeze, afraid to spoil that lovely blank page (or blank screen) with a cheap parody of the masterpiece you envision in your head.

Remember, you can't argue with yourself; the best approach is pure deception. When I am stuck on trying to make it perfect, I just tell myself I'm going to write a lousy version and get it out of my system, so I'm free to write the perfect version. Later, of course, I find that it just takes a bit of editing and rewriting of the lousy version to come up with something astoundingly close to how I envisioned the perfect version—but I don't worry about that at the time. I have to truly convince myself (and this isn't just tricking myself, because it's true) that I *can't* write the perfect version until the lousy version is done.

2. **Something is wrong with your approach.** Maybe you don't want to write because, instinctively, you know you're taking a wrong turn. But since you don't know the right way to go, you're feeling like a friend of mine who said about his writing, "I am stalled on the side of the highway, looking for miles in both directions, with no cars in sight."

The solution to this is in the joke about the old farmer who gave directions by saying, "You can't get there from here; you've got to go someplace else first." Keep writing what you're writing until you see *why* it's wrong; you may even find it *isn't* wrong, after all.

Or, if that's too frustrating, try a new approach. Novelists sometimes write scenes that they are *not* going to include in their stories, just as an experiment—perhaps to explore a character's personality, or a plot twist they had previously discarded. You can do this in nonfiction as well. Write about a tangential subject that you were not planning to use in the book. Amazingly, such counterintuitive actions can often get you unstuck—and maybe even give you fodder for a new article or book!

Of course, we all rebel against this kind of wasted effort of writing, starting over, and rewriting material we expect to discard. But that leads to another reason you don't want to write:

3. **It's too much work.** Come on, admit it: there's a little bit of the sluggard from the book of Proverbs in all of us. After all, deep down in our hearts we all harbor a secret desire to find a shortcut to success. For the past thirty years, I've been looking for an easier writing method, but it's beginning to dawn on me that there isn't one.

Keep plugging away and resist your internal sloth; eventually you will reach a point of no return in a writing project where it's easier to finish the job than to quit and say, "Look at all the time and energy I've wasted." My brother, a writer of fiction, says most people stall on a novel at thirty pages or so. If they get to one hundred pages, they figure they've invested so much in it that they have to finish it—and they usually do! (Have you noticed how many examples I have from *fiction* writers about writers' block? I suppose we nonfiction people can comfort ourselves with the knowledge that novelists seem to get their creative juices clogged up even worse than we do!)

4. **Writing is too scary.** Behind most of the other reasons you don't want to write is plain old fear: fear of working too hard, fear of failure, fear of doing it wrong—fear, fear, fear. But remember what Moses told Joshua as he was about to enter the Promised Land: "Be strong and of good courage!" You are about to enter the Promised Land of the writing world—a finished manuscript!—but to win that new territory, you have to battle the giants of the land: perfectionism, slothfulness, and especially fear. There is a battle ahead, but with God's grace you can take the land. Be strong and of good courage!

Still Stuck? Here Are Some Ideas

Even after you have built up a creative pressure through brainstorming, research, outlining, and proposal writing, it is still possible to find yourself staring at a blank page until you think you're going to scream. These suggestions may help:

1. **Bathe your book project in prayer.** You need to get a group of people praying for you and your book project. I can't emphasize this more strongly, but I also don't see any need to explain *why* you should get a group of prayer partners—you *know* why. I'm just here to remind you.

2. **Don't be afraid to go back to the drawing board.** It may be that any writing block you have in working on the first draft is due to a lack of depth in your earlier steps: brainstorming, researching, outlining. You may have done enough prep work to put together a passable proposal, but not enough to prepare

a first draft. So go ahead and rethink your outline, dig up some more information, toss a few ideas around. Don't think of it as retracing your steps, because the process is not necessarily chronological, remember. It may shock you to discover that some writers return to these earlier steps even at the *revision* stage.

If you haven't figured this out already, brainstorming, researching, and outlining are going to become familiar friends throughout the process of writing your book. You may as well learn to enjoy it! Revisiting these three steps helps you regain a fresh perspective on the topic, and brings back to mind all the loose ends of the topic that you wanted to follow up on. And the best part is that you don't have to review the research for the entire book at once, but only for the particular chapter you are working on—which brings me to the next point:

3. **Work on a chapter at a time.** Remind yourself that you don't have to write the whole book at once. As obvious as that may sound, it's easy to forget it when you are faced with that intimidating blank page. Even an individual chapter may seem daunting, but you can break it down into manageable steps. How? Well, that brings me to my fourth point.

4. **Refer to your outline and the chapter-by-chapter synopsis in your proposal; let them work for you.** The outline (which you have been continually refining, right?) should be getting detailed enough that you can identify separate pieces of the chapter and work on each of those. I start my draft of a chapter with its paragraph description from the synopsis at the top of the page. With that staring me in the

face, I don't stray from what the chapter is supposed to be about; after all, the paragraph is the crux of the chapter in a nutshell—at least, it is if you did your synopsis well.

If the outline is not helping you to get started, then write an expansion of the chapter synopsis, bringing in some of the research you've gathered, etc. Then write a further expansion on that material—maybe you'll add an opening anecdote, include a few biblical references, or make your concluding point stronger. Then expand on the synopsis again, and again, and again—as many times as it takes to round out the chapter. It is amazing how this method can cause a chapter to appear before your eyes. But there's another thing to remember that will help you see your rough draft through to the end.

5. **Remember, it's a rough draft, not a final draft.** If you're a perfectionist about your writing, now is the time to get over it. You can't expect perfection at this point. Don't worry if it isn't quite right yet. You want to write a book in the worst possible way? Here's your chance! Decide ahead of time that your rough draft is going to be pretty awful, and join the ranks of the great writers of the world. (Hemingway, for example, described his first drafts in quite "colorful" language.) Save the niceties for the revision stage.

I can say that over and over, but I know you are still going to hit an occasional paragraph, sentence, or phrase that you feel you just *have to* rework until it's right. If you don't control that urge, you'll waste precious time worrying over it like a dog with a bone. A technique that I've found helpful for those problem sections of a rough draft is to write myself notes in brackets [like this]. If I can't seem to say what I want to say, or I know my argument's weak, I write in brackets how I want to change it later, such as: [find a better way to phrase this] or [think this concept through a little more]. The brackets help me to tell my internal "editor" to shut up while I'm writing.

"That Reminds Me of a Story . . ."

The first draft should also be where you begin to populate your manuscript with stories—stories that illustrate a point, anchor a truth in your mind, or put some human flesh on a principle. We call these little narrative events anecdotes.

Most of us know someone who is prone to interrupt the flow of a pleasant conversation with the words, "That reminds me of a story..."—usually accompanied by stifled groans and a general squirming of the audience in their seats. And what follows is an old chestnut that everyone's already heard a dozen times or a pointless, rambling tale that wanders off into a forest of verbiage and ends up nowhere in particular.

It seems like there's one in every family. (And if you can't think of someone like that in your family, have you considered that it could be *you*?)

But when my father was "reminded of a story," all ears perked up. Everyone knew they were in for a tale laced with humor, drama, and suspense, often ending with an ironic twist. They might even learn something in the process. The difference, of course, was the storyteller as much as the story. The power of a tale is often in the telling.

But the popularity of my father's anecdotes can't all be explained away by his delivery. It was the content of his stories as well. Most were original, and all had one thing in common: each centered on a particular point, and the thrust of the story drove home that truth. That is one of the best pieces of writing advice my dad ever taught me.

You'll frequently hear nonfiction writing instructors counsel their students to sprinkle their material with illustrations and anecdotes. While it is a sound recommendation, it can often do more harm than good if a story is not chosen carefully. Your anecdote has to drive home a single truth—clearly and unambiguously—and do it in a memorable way.

Unfortunately, some anecdotes are a little *too* memorable; they've been published repeatedly until they have lost their power. The story of the old violin and "the touch of the master's hand" is an example of a great illustration that has been dulled by overuse. Some anecdotes can become the victim of their own success! So use anecdotes, but remember that nothing beats the freshness of originality.

Choosing the right story is difficult, even for the best of communicators. A speech by a seminary president began with the story of an invading army that captured a nobleman's home. The servants fled, leaving the nobleman's infant son to the mercy of his enemies. Fortunately, the family's pet baboon sensed the danger, picked up the baby and climbed atop a steeple so the invaders could not harm him. The grateful father put an image of the baboon on the family crest and added the words, "Not unmindful of his kindness." The president concluded by saying he was "not unmindful of God's kindness" in his life.

Aside from the unfortunate comparison of God to a baboon, there is a wider issue at stake here. Is this story a good illustration of remembering God's kindness? It would be better used as an illustration of the amazing ability of animals to sense danger—or even as an explanation of how strange images can sometimes end up on a family crest. Your story should make the point you want to make so clearly that you don't have to explain it.

One book I edited told how the mink is such a scrupulously clean animal that poachers can capture it by blocking the entrance to its lair with dirt and filth. The mink will allow itself to be caught rather than risk getting its coat soiled. The author concluded that Christians should be just as scrupulous about avoiding the filth of sin. I couldn't help it—when I read that, I thought, *So if I avoid sin, I'll be captured and killed?* Make sure your illustration has no double meaning.

Sometimes, of course, the value of a tale really is in the way it's told; you can often salvage an illustration by a bit of skillful rewording. The author of the mink story solved his problem by adding, "While physical cleanliness for the mink can result in its death, for the Christian, spiritual cleanliness leads to life and peace." It's also helpful to keep your stories as short and succinct as possible. Even the best illustration can fall flat if the point gets lost in the verbosity.

Strive for originality in your anecdotes. That doesn't mean you should *never* use published illustrations, but if it's from a best-selling book, it's likely to have been told and retold. Should you use illustrations from your own experience? Absolutely! But also include stories from others; it helps your writing relate to a wider audience and prevents it from being overly autobiographical. By bringing in others' stories, you add an air of objectivity and show how God works with different people.

You can pick up stories in personal conversation or by e-mail, asking friends to share their experiences on a particular topic. (Of course, you need to get their permission to use it.) Many authors have produced great books through this kind of informal survey. Mary Tatem interviewed over one hundred women for her book, *Just Call Me Mom! Practical Steps to Becoming a Better Mother-in-Law*. The resulting manuscript was much more readable and authoritative, because we heard from dozens of mothers-in-law and daughters-in-law, not just one.

So use illustrations in your writing. Just be sure to choose them carefully, and you'll avoid the stifled groans and shifting seats.

"Just the Facts, Ma'am"—Using Description Wisely

Anecdotes, as well as genres that involve storytelling (memoir, biography, and even devotional), call for the use of *fiction techniques* in the nonfiction book. My mentor in this area is Officer Joe Friday from the old TV show *Dragnet*. He was a no-nonsense kind of guy. He didn't let crime victims go on and on about their feelings; his motto was "Just the facts, Ma'am." And that's the attitude you need to take when you want to put more description in your writing.

Don't get me wrong, you can't ignore emotion. Emotional response is a key to your writing. Dwight V. Swain says it this way: "The application of language to the manipulation of reader feelings... [is] the foundation stone on which you as a writer stand or fall."[1] It's a question of empathy. You want the reader to feel the emotions and sensations along with you—or along with your characters, if it's fiction.

But exactly *how* do you bring empathy into your writing? You do it by description. You've probably heard this referred to as the "show, don't tell" concept. You don't *tell* the reader what they should be feeling, you *show* them the emotion, and let them feel it themselves.

Ironically, however, you can't do it directly, by simply expressing feelings or emotions, because then you become like Joe Friday's crime victim, blubbering all over his shoes. And the reader feels like Friday—a detached observer. But it's you, the writer, who needs to be the detached observer, describing passion dispassionately, building on the details to the point that you spark the reader's natural ability to empathize, to experience the emotion vicariously.

What I'm saying is, if I try to "describe" emotions, I find that I'm "telling" them; but if I describe physical reactions, body language, etc. (the little, easily ignored details), then I'm "showing." It's the irony that if you hyper-focus on trying to be "healthy" you can end up a hypochondriac. But if you focus on getting enough sleep, eating right, exercising, etc. (the little, easily ignored details), you'll find you end up being healthy without even trying.

One thing I have learned that helped me improve my descriptions is to concentrate on verbs in the sentence, rather than adjectives (despite the fact that adjectives are defined as "descriptive" words). Not that I ignore adjectives—or nouns, or adverbs—but simply that the descriptive power often seems to be centered in verbs. If you notice, your strongest verbs really make descriptions sing. But when most of your sentences have weak verbs like *has* or *is*, the power is lost. If you say, for example, that the bird's feathers *exploded* with color, or that the constant chatter in the room *engulfed* the normally dead quiet, it is more effective.

Learning to be more observant of the world around you is good training for developing descriptions that are fresh and vivid. I don't think very many of us really observe life that carefully, and as a result, our descriptions become trite—such as "fingers dancing across the keyboard." It's impossible for anyone to be completely original, but when you use an image, a simile, a metaphor, try something that is not the first thing the reader will expect. For example, if I said, "I'm as hungry as a . . ." you are probably thinking "horse," right? But if I said, "I'm as hungry as a supermodel on a diet," I'd probably surprise you, wouldn't I?

John Grisham is great at this. Take this excerpt from *Bleachers*: "He looked twice as big now, his neck as thick as an oak stump, his shoulders as wide as a door. His biceps and triceps were many times the normal size. His stomach looked like a cobblestone street." [2] Grisham's similes are great, aren't they? If someone's going to be trite, it's probably going to be a simile, for some reason. But Grisham knows how to make every sentence bright and fresh.

I like how the psalmists use concrete images like "He breaks the bow" in Psalm 46 to say that God destroys a nation's ability to make war. The psalmists tend to mix very down-to-earth statements with soaring imagery. If you want to look into more of the poetic techniques used by the psalmists and other biblical writers, check out *How to Read the Bible for All Its Worth*.[3]

When using imagery for God, it is critical that it be solidly grounded in Scripture. It can be easy to develop a simile or extend a metaphor and yet not necessarily say anything truthful about God. It's no good saying that you are using poetic license; your comparison still has to have a biblical foundation. Fred Hartley, in the booklet, *Holy Spirit, Fill Me*, said that when he was a teenager he thought the Holy Spirit was "like a giant computer . . . like a nuclear power plant in the sky . . . like the Force in Star Wars." He later added, "Fortunately, my concept has since been corrected by careful Bible teaching. . . . Far more than simply being a power or an impersonal force, He [the Holy Spirit] is just as much a real, live, distinct Person as you and I."[4] That doesn't mean, of course, that you cannot use a comparison that the biblical writers don't use. It just means that your comparison has to have connotations that jive with Scripture.

Turning Your Preaching or Speaking into Writing

Are you a preacher or teacher? Do you do public speaking of any sort? If so, you no doubt have considered how you might put the content of your messages, lectures, workshops, etc. into written form.

On the surface, doing so appears to be a simple matter. A well-prepared and well-delivered message can simply be transcribed and published with little or no revision, right? What could be easier?

A quick reading of an actual transcription will soon dispel that myth. Most of us fail to realize how much the force of our personalities carries our speaking over such obstacles as wordiness, bad grammar, poor logic, and confusing arrangement of material. Added to that is the mystique of the spoken word: it has its own unique strengths and weaknesses, and the transition from oral presentation to the printed page is rarely seamless.

One proof that transcripts can lose something in the translation is the written material from stand-up comics. I've always admired the comedy of Bob Hope, but I've read his attempts to put his jokes on paper, and the result is dismal. (Conversely, I don't think Alan King was ever very funny as a stand-up comedian, but his books were hilarious!)

If you are ready to accept that moving from speaking to writing involves some work, where do you start? Start with a transcript, and work on boiling it down from the natural verbosity of the spoken word. Next, try to outline the material—see if you can follow the logical progression of thought from the beginning of the message through to the end. (One simple way to do this is to write a synopsis—three or four words—of each paragraph in the margin of the transcript.) You may be surprised to discover how seemingly disjointed your own speaking is.

This doesn't necessarily mean you are a bad speaker; in fact, it may be evidence of being a good speaker—one who instinctively reads the audience, identifies when they are confused, and repeats or reinforces a point when needed. In written form, of course, you don't want this kind of repetition; you want to avoid confusing the reader in the first place. There may be places in a transcript where you have to do some serious rewriting in order to keep the reader's attention and help them follow your train of thought.

Another problem with a transcript is that much of a spoken presentation is the reverse of a written presentation: for example, a preacher often makes a point, and then illustrates it with an anecdote; an author is more likely to tell the anecdote first, and then point out what the anecdote illustrates.

In some cases, you'll have to explain some things at more length or drastically rephrase them in written form. I'm talking about situations such as when the spoken presentation includes a visual which the reader cannot see (a picture truly is worth a thousand words!), or where vocal inflection carries most of the meaning. Usually, however, most of your job will involve cutting down the wordiness of the transcript.

Single messages generally have enough content for a chapter, and multiple messages may be enough to comprise a book. However, if you are trying to build a manuscript from a sermon series or multiple workshops, be sure there is a strong theme that connects all the messages, or it won't hold together as a unit. A collection of *unrelated* sermons will never sell as a book—that is, unless your name is Chuck Swindoll or Charles Stanley.

Turning your taped messages into books can be an excellent way to recycle your material and present it to a wider audience. Just be prepared to do a bit of work when you translate it from voice to paper.

What to Do When You're Done

Now, once you've completed your rough draft, you'll be tempted to have everyone look at it. *Don't do it!* You'll get responses that are likely to discourage you—and unnecessarily so. Remember, it's *supposed* to be lousy—it's your first draft! However, even though it's not great, it probably contains most of the basic features of what you envisioned for your book.

Give yourself a small reward with the completion of each chapter, then a big reward when the whole thing is done. Finally—and I know this sounds terrible—when it's all done, don't even look at it for a solid week. A week later, you can look at the manuscript (yes, that's right—you have a manuscript!) with a fresh perspective.

In the meantime, you might show the draft to *one or two* people—but only if they are experienced enough at writing to understand what a rough draft is all about, and wise enough to give you some useful feedback (which you will *not* look at until about a week later). Your rough draft reviewer probably should look at the outline and proposal of your book as well, so they can see if the manuscript is going in the direction you planned to take it. (It is amazing how blind we writers can be. I've sometimes taken chapters off on tangents, but never really noticed until an objective party pointed it out to me.)

If you follow the suggestions in this chapter, and put a little sweat into it, you should have a complete first draft. (I meant that as a joke, you know; "complete first draft" is a contradiction in terms.) It's probably a real disappointment: filled with bad grammar and syntax, nowhere near the number of words you promised in your proposal, and (in some parts, at least) just plain dull—terribly dull. But it's your baby—an ugly baby, no doubt, but it's yours.

I will say it again: your first draft may seem pretty awful, but it's not supposed to be perfect—it's a *first draft*! Let go of perfectionism and celebrate!

Don't rest on your laurels, though; next comes revision.

FIRST DRAFT TIP #1:

If you have enough interest in a subject to write a book about it, chances are you have already written *something* about it—even if it's only a comment on Facebook or an e-mail to a friend. That raw material may be a good start for at least one chapter of your draft.

FIRST DRAFT TIP #2:

You probably want to write the draft of your first chapter first, but there is nothing wrong with writing the remaining chapters out of order. If you are stuck on chapter three, start working on four or five.

FIRST DRAFT TIP #3:

If you are of the sermonic persuasion (a preacher), you may habitually break down every argument into three points, each point starting with a particular letter. This rarely works as well on paper as it does in a sermon, so try to relax the alliteration; your readers will bless you for it.

CHAPTER 7 *VANDEMARK*

REVISION: WHERE THE REAL WRITING STARTS

I'm not a very good writer, but I'm an excellent rewriter.

— James Michener

O would some power the gift to give us

To see ourselves as others see us!

It would from many a blunder free us,

And foolish notion.

— Robert Burns

Start revising your manuscript a week after you finish that first draft. Don't wait much longer than that, or you'll lose your momentum. Don't try it much sooner than that, or you may not have the perspective you need—because now you are going to start looking at your writing as if someone else wrote it.

Can you really do that? Who knows? But you have to try. Later in this chapter we'll discuss how to do self-editing, by which I mean the finer points of revision—reviewing the rough draft in a paragraph-by-paragraph, sentence-by-sentence, word-by-word process.

First, however, you need to see the "big picture": Do the chapters individually, and the manuscript as a whole, fit together logically and smoothly? Have you missed any major component of the topic you are writing on? Have you included anything that is extraneous? In this vein, I'd like to quote from Giovanni Papini, author of *The Life of Christ*:

> Most people think that to make a book it is enough to have an idea and then to take so many words and put them together. Not so. A kiln of tiles, a pile of rocks, are not a house. To build up a house, to build up a book, to build up a soul, are undertakings which require all of a man's power. . . . Only when he has finished a book does an author know how he should have written it. When he has set down the last word, he ought to turn back, begin at the beginning, and do it all over again with the experience acquired in the work.[1]

Personally, I think Papini simply enjoyed torturing himself, but he has a point. You've learned a few things in the writing of this book; don't save this knowledge for the next book you write—you may never get a second chance if you don't put your best into this one. Put everything you can into this book, even if it means you have to go back to square one. In other words—and I may sound like a broken record at this point—you need to go back to the beginning steps of brainstorming, researching, and outlining. In this case, however, I would not advise that you do all three at once.

Start with your outline. Skim over the rough draft and compare it to the outline. Are there discrepancies? Does your outline (or the chapter synopsis from your proposal, for that matter) include anything that is *missing* from the rough draft—or vice versa? If so, you need to decide *why*. Did you simply fail to follow the outline? Or, as Papini has noted, perhaps you learned something in the process of writing the draft that changed your understanding. At any rate, identify any missing or extraneous material, and make a judgment call to add it in or take it out.

One example of how the writing of the draft can lead you to change your outline was in my book on Thomas Barnardo, *Father to Nobody's Children*. I had in my outline a rather long chapter on Barnardo's legal battles. I shortened and simplified that chapter in making my draft because the book was written for a preteen audience, and I realized in the writing of the chapter that the legal issues were too complex to discuss in detail.

Along with accidental omissions, you may have deliberate ones. Remember those bracketed ([ ]) portions of the manuscript that I mentioned in writing the rough draft—those places where you needed to add or fix something, but couldn't put your finger on it? By now, as Papini says, you may have a better idea what to say and how to say it. And, with the perspective of the whole manuscript behind you, it may be clear that some of those bracketed notes or sections, which at the time seemed indispensable, are not really needed after all—no matter *what* the original outline says.

You may even decide to *rethink* your outline, now that you're looking at it from a different point in the process. Now that you can see how the chapters unfold, you may decide that it's better to change the order of the chapters, expand one chapter into two, or merge two chapters into one. If major surgery is in order, *do it now*. Better to decide now than to decide it after you've finished the *final* version! But don't do those kinds of major structural revisions without mapping them out. Work out your revisions in outline form *first*, and then use the revised outline as a *writing plan* (where have I heard *that* before?). I guarantee you that the revisions will be faster and less painful if you map out the changes ahead of time.

Restructuring, reordering or even *deleting* chapters may be necessary, but don't make such decisions lightly. When you put together your original outline, you may have been smarter than you thought. Introductory chapters and certain explanatory sections may seem repetitious to you now, but after all, you've been eating, sleeping, and probably dreaming this book for months—but of course, the reader hasn't. Don't lose your perspective! Try to look at the book as if you don't know anything about the topic, as if someone else wrote it.

Also remember that if you make major structural changes, you have to double-check your text for wording that is based on the *old* structure. For example, your text may read, "In the previous chapter, we discussed . . ." If you changed the order of the chapters, it may have to read, "In the *next* chapter we *will* discuss . . ."

Developing your book's structure is an art—no one can tell you how to make these decisions; you have to do it yourself. So I'm not suggesting that major structural changes are inevitable. You may conclude that your rough draft is not too bad as-is—and if you've done a good job on your outline, that should come as no surprise. Just make sure you aren't trying to avoid the hard work of restructuring.

Finally, in all of this rethinking about the structure of the book, keep your perspective and realize that the average reader is not enough of a logical thinker to notice. (If more people could think logically, half of the books in the world would not be necessary.) Besides, you really don't want your book's structure to be all that obvious, anyway. The skeleton should be *under* the skin.

Return to researching and brainstorming. If you hit a portion of the rough draft that needs work or is lacking something, yet you are stuck as to how to change or add to it, that's a signal that it's time to return to *researching*. Perhaps a little digging will snag you an essential nugget of information or a pithy quote that you missed the first time around. Maybe you'll even need to return to *brainstorming*, so that you have a chance to rethink the problem and identify an entirely new facet to the issue.

More than One Way to Say It

When you are having trouble revising your manuscript, however, it's often a result of a chronic mentality that says, "The way I wrote it the first time is the best." Don't tell me you've *never* thought that, because all writers do at some time or another. It was my biggest bugaboo—until I attended a writer's conference with Sherwood Wirt, who was at that time editor of *Decision* magazine. He showed us an exercise that trains your mind in how to attack the passages that defy revision. It freed me forever from the subconscious "it's right the first time" attitude. Here it is:

1. Write about an incident in your life, or a truth that you have learned, and describe it in three hundred words.

2. Identify what portion of your short essay is the "beginning." Probably it's the first two to four sentences. Write five new beginnings for the essay.

3. Identify what portion of your short essay is the "ending." Write five new endings.

4. Finally, take the best of the six beginnings and endings (I'll betcha it's not the *first* ones you wrote) and *expand* your essay to roughly double its size—five hundred to six hundred words.

This exercise is hard work, but it's worth it. It will literally change the way you write.

Let me give you a way to approach the fourth step of the exercise: you may find it easy to expand the piece by gleaning from your previously written beginnings and endings, since in creating them you may have done more than simply reword. I often discover in my rewriting that I've introduced new information that I failed to mention the first time. That way, nothing is wasted.

Speaking of not wasting anything, now that you have written a short essay of five hundred to six hundred words, why don't you submit it somewhere and get it published? After all that rewriting, it's probably one of the best pieces you've ever done!

How to Edit Your Own Material

Revising your manuscript for publication will inevitably put you in the uncomfortable position of editing your own material. Even if you hire a freelance editor to "pre-edit" your material before submitting it (which is a fine thing to do, as long as you choose a good editor), you will need to review the editorial changes that were made—a process that is not much different from self-editing, anyway!

What makes self-editing so difficult is a basic fact of human nature: we tend to be blind to our own mistakes. (Otherwise, we wouldn't keep making the same ones repeatedly!) What is needed is a way to step out of your skin—to be objective in the truest sense of the word. Robert Burns had that in mind when he asked for the gift to "see ourselves as others see us." How do you develop the ability to "see yourself as others see you"—or at least, as the reader sees you?

A second problem with editing your material is based on the way our brains work. When we do editing, we are working with an entirely different part of our brain than when we are writing. (And sometimes we don't use our brains at all, but that's another issue.) As a result, a good writer may not necessarily be a good editor, because it is a different kind of skill.

Are these problems insurmountable? Not at all—you just have to follow a few rules:

1. **Sleep on it.** Don't try to edit your masterpiece while the creative fire is still warm. Lay it aside and don't even think about it for a couple days. Then you can look at it as if it were someone else's material.

2. **Do multiple passes.** Go through once for proofreading (grammar, syntax, and punctuation), once as an overview for the general thrust of the message, and once for the literary power of individual paragraphs, sentences, and words. In that

last pass, read each sentence twice before moving on to the next sentence. My editor on this book, Vie Herlocker, suggests a separate pass for what she calls "weed words"—overused words and phrases. Everyone has their own pet phrases that they use and reuse—and reuse. ("A lot" is one of my bad habits.) Compile a list of your own weed words, then do a search for them—and be merciless!

3. **Experiment.** Cross out some words at random. Re-punctuate a sentence. Move some paragraphs around. When you finish your experimentation, review the result. Does it work? If not, go back to the way it was. But there are times when random changes can force you to look at the writing differently.

4. **Rewrite when necessary—and even when it's not necessary.** Rewrite the beginning, the ending, or other passages from a different viewpoint—even if you are satisfied with the original. Remember, you can always return to the old version if you don't like the new one.

This sounds suspiciously like Sherwood Wirt's writing exercise, doesn't it? That's because the intent is the same—to help you get past the mentality that says there is only one way to say something. (Even the Bible tells the same story different ways.) Beginning writers often think that their first try at expressing something is perfect. A professional writer knows that you almost never get something right the first time.

5. **Finally, pray for objectivity—for eyes to "see ourselves as others see us."** Ask the Lord to help you be ruthless in your

revisions. Sir Arthur Quiller-Couch, in warning authors against the use of "extraneous ornament" in their writing, gave this harshly worded advice: "Whenever you feel an impulse to perpetrate a piece of exceptionally fine writing, obey it—whole-heartedly—and delete it before sending your manuscript to press. *Murder your darlings.*" [2] (I am tempted to soften that advice, but perhaps that's one of my own little "darlings" I need to put out of its misery.)

Along with these general rules for self-editing are some practical tips for specific situations:

Narration

In narration (especially biographical or anecdotal material) that is *spatial* (involving people moving through a building or neighborhood, for instance), draw yourself a diagram—not for publication, but for your own reference. Better yet, ask someone else to read the passage and draw the diagram. I edited a fiction book that had a character going up and down stairs so much that I lost track of where he was—and since he was breaking into his enemy's castle to rescue a princess, his location was important to the plot!

Terminology

Watch out for terminology. It is amazing how the context and connotations of words, the slightest shades of meaning, can twist what you are trying to say into something totally different. For example, I wrote a news article about a local church that had a vision to become a "major missionary organization." That has a connotation of being an independent group, which was not true at all. I changed it to "major missions base" and the story read better. Only one person in a hundred might have gotten the wrong impression by that phrase, but if several of those bloopers compound themselves in your book, you may find yourself in trouble.

Punctuation

If you never use certain punctuation marks, then you aren't using all the tools available to you. Some punctuation allows you to say things without resorting to wordiness, bad grammar, or fractured syntax. Frequent and repeated use of a certain punctuation mark should also be suspect. It may imply that you are being too repetitious in your sentence structure, or it may simply be the result of using punctuation incorrectly.

If these suggestions make you feel paranoid about your writing, be thankful. A healthy dose of paranoia is an editor's best friend. When you edit, you must question every little thing. Just learn when to turn the paranoia on and off. The critical, questioning eye of an editor only gets in your way when you are writing a first draft. If you don't learn to turn off the editor within you when you write, you'll find yourself fighting and squelching the free flow of your words. You have to learn to take off your editor's hat when you write, or you're headed for a terminal case of writer's block.

Developing your self-editing skills can greatly improve your writing—and greatly improve your chances of being published. A self-edited manuscript makes life easier for the editor and ultimately for the reader. It's a way to apply the Golden Rule to your own material.

Parts and Pieces

Why do publishers reject proposals with no feedback except the vague but popular "Doesn't fit our needs at this time"? Why do editors tell authors that a particular chapter in their book "needs work"—but they don't say what work it needs?

This kind of feedback is often an indicator of a problem in the general flow of the text: the reader repeatedly encounters communication roadblocks that make the writing hard to read. There is not just *one* problem with the manuscript, but a bunch of little ones—almost imperceptible errors that have a cumulative effect.

How do you find these little glitches? Do what editors do (when they have time!): dissect the material into parts and pieces.

Let's look at the parts and pieces of a chapter, starting from largest to smallest:

Sections

Take a wide-angle lens to your writing to identify individual sections. Look at its basic structure—how you start the chapter, where you take it, and how you wrap it up. That, of course, is the most basic of structures: the beginning, the middle, and the end. Your chapter may have a more complex structure, but it will always include these three elements.

By identifying the sections, you may discover that you've neglected an entire step in logic or a certain facet of the topic. Perhaps you need to begin the chapter on a stronger note, or wrap it up with a more definite solution.

Paragraphs

Too many writers, it seems, pay too little attention to where they start a paragraph. This is a waste of a valuable tool that makes writing flow logically. A paragraph needs to be one or more sentences that all have the same theme, so that the paragraph conveys a single idea.

I like to go through a piece of writing and put a brief summary (three or four words) of each paragraph in the margin. It helps me identify what paragraphs are failing to convey a single idea. It also helps me see problems in the flow of the material. I tend to be the type of writer that jumps around logically, and labeling paragraphs helps me keep my non-linear, stream-of-consciousness thinking under control.

Sentences

Sentences are a key to your writing style and structure. Structurally, you need to view the sentence in the context of its paragraph. The first sentence in a paragraph often introduces or summarizes the idea of the paragraph. The first sentence may also be a transition—it moves the reader from one topic to another. ("My daughter then asked me…" is an example of a transition.) Transition sentences are especially important when you start a new section of a chapter.

The remaining sentences in a paragraph are supposed to build on the main idea. If the sentences within the paragraph do not relate to each other, your writing will be very difficult to read. Readers can only keep one idea in their heads at a time, and if you have three sentences in a row, each introducing a new idea, you drive your readers crazy!

Stylistically, sentences help put variety in your writing. The contrast between sentences that are simple and complex, short and long, can produce a very pleasing effect. A healthy balance of length and complexity in your sentences varies the rhythm and keeps the reader interested. When all the sentences in a paragraph are short, simple ones, it makes the paragraph seem choppy. When they are all long and complex, it's too hard to read.

Words

Variety in the use of individual words is good, too. Don't always use the first word you think of; try something different. Make it a practice to look up words in the dictionary, even ones you think you know. You may want to use two different dictionaries, just to be sure you understand the exact shade of meaning.

Don't go overboard with twenty-dollar words, however. One Christian author I really admire makes the mistake (in my opinion) of over-using his thesaurus. Occasionally, he will include a sentence with an odd word in it—a synonym for a simple word like "tree" or "walk." When he should have used the simple word, he uses the twenty-dollar word, and it sounds awkward, because it has a fine shade of meaning that doesn't fit the context.

When you find an error in grammar, punctuation, typography, or incorrect use of a word, do a search to see if you have repeated that same error in other places in the manuscript. (My editor discovered, much to my chagrin, that I used "Here's some" several times instead of "Here are some.")

Breaking down your writing into parts and pieces is difficult and challenging, but it can be very rewarding. Frankly, very few writers bother to go to all this trouble, but those who do are more likely to have publishers respond with a contract rather than a rejection slip.

Removing the Excess Baggage

For quite a while, I had a box full of odds and ends in the trunk of my car. I don't exactly remember when or where I picked all this stuff up, but most of it was useless. I was just too lazy to throw it all away. Besides, it was easy to forget about the box when I didn't open my trunk for days at a time.

I finally got rid of the box (at least, I *think* I did—maybe I should check) because it caused so many problems. It was always in the way whenever I went shopping or packed for a trip. And the thing was so heavy it was like carrying around an extra passenger all the time, so I probably wasted a ton of gas. (Yes, Mr. Gore, it's all my fault the polar ice caps are melting!)

When it comes to writing (you were probably wondering when I was going to get around to that), you may have your own box-full of excess cargo in your manuscript. I'm talking about verbosity, redundancy, prolixity—in a word, uh, well, *wordiness*.

This is what editors are for, you may say. And you would be right. There have been times that I have edited a book to two-thirds its length, without much more than clearing away the excess words. But this takes time and effort. When a publisher is offered the choice between a wordy but good manuscript and a succinct and good manuscript, which one do you think gets the green light?

So consider your manuscript like a rocket to the moon, in which every ounce of excess weight has to go; or like a bus, where every passenger must pay to ride. Any words that don't pay their fare are off at the next corner. How do you identify your non-paying passengers? Here are a few places to look:

Passive voice: You can save a multitude of words by looking for any form of "to be" (such as "is," "was," "has been") followed by a participle (mostly, verbs that end in "ing" or "ed").

"He stabbed me!" is what a guy might cry just before he collapses with a knife in his back. It has a nice, direct ring to it (and there's nothing like a knife in your back to help you be succinct).

Can you see this same guy collapse on the floor and say with his dying breath, "I have been stabbed by him"? Or worse yet, "A stabbing event has been personally experienced by me, which was caused by him"?

I'm not saying you should *never* use passive voice; just be frugal with it. Use it when it's simpler to emphasize the object of a sentence (the thing being acted upon), and not the subject (the one doing the action). I might say, for example, "The money was stolen" if I didn't know who stole it.

Transitions: When you finish making a point in a chapter and want to move on to the next point, it is common to include a transition, such as "On the other hand . . ." or "This is why . . ." There is nothing wrong with transitions—in fact, they can be critical sometimes—but like any good thing they can also be overdone. (This is where you can find many of your weed words.)

One kind of transition that is a waste of words is the explanation that follows a Scripture verse. It typically begins with, "This passage says…" and is followed by a drab rephrasing of the verse that was just read. This practice is common in transcribed (and barely edited) sermons. We have just read the passage, so we don't need to be told what it says. It insults the reader's intelligence. When this kind of transition is used in a sermon, we recognize the redundancy as a verbal cue that keeps us on track with the speaker. But we don't need this kind of repetition in writing, because we can always reread a previous sentence if we lose track of where we are.

Paragraphs with redundant sentences: The sentences in a paragraph must be related to each other, as I noted earlier, but this is very different from what you may have learned in school. I remember being taught to begin a paragraph with a summary sentence, followed by two or three sentences that do little more than rephrase or reiterate the first sentence. What a recipe for redundancy! It usually results in a paragraph of three or four sentences that all say the same thing. If your first sentence says everything you want to say in the paragraph, move on—trust me, your reader will bless you for it.

Rabbit trails: As you search for ways to trim your manuscript, be on the lookout for places where you went off on a tangent and strayed from the real thrust of the chapter. If you aren't sure whether a point you are making in a chapter is needed, it probably isn't. But you can verify that by re-outlining the chapter to see if every point you make fits in the overall pattern.

These are just a few of the things to look for if you want to remove wordiness from your manuscript. If there is any single secret to successful writing, avoiding wordiness is it.

By the way, I just checked the trunk of my car—*the box is still there.*

Maintaining Logical Flow

When I was a college student, taking my car to be repaired was truly an educational experience. My mechanic felt it was his duty to explain everything in detail, in a monologue punctuated frequently by, "Ya follow me?" A typical lecture would begin like this: "So the gas goes into the carburetor, ya follow me? And it mixes with the air, ya follow me?"

While I don't recommend such repetition in writing, my mechanic had the right idea. You need to make sure your audience follows you from one sentence to the next. This is what we call logical flow.

Proper connection between sentences prevents what logicians call a *non sequitur* (literally, "it does not follow"), where one sentence is followed by a second that does not have a direct logical connection to the previous one. For example, one submitted manuscript I received had this passage: "Humility encompasses all of life. It is not a mask you put on to hide who you really are." Well, both of those statements may be true, but do they logically connect with one another?

Well, not directly. The first sentence says that humility encompasses all of life; the second sentence says it is not a "mask. . . to hide who you really are." Why is something that is all encompassing unable to "hide who you really are?" I could have an attitude of pretentiousness that encompasses all of my life, and it actually *would* be a mask to hide who I really am!

While the mask idea also implies something you put on and take off (i.e., *not* integrated into all of life), that logical connection is overshadowed by the connotation of "falseness" in the metaphor of a mask. It is true that if humility is not integrated into your life it is false humility, but that logical step *is never stated outright by the author*, only assumed. The subtle break in logical flow causes the reader to lose their connection with you. Wouldn't it be better to make the second sentence something like, "It is not like a pair of shoes you can put on and take off; that is not true humility, but a false mask"?

Sometimes the problem, strictly speaking, is not *logical* flow, but *chronological* flow—and the example I'll give is from my own writing. Here's what I originally wrote at the end of a submission checklist for authors:

> Near the end of our editing, typesetting, and proofreading process, we will send you a galley copy of the complete typeset manuscript for your review. You will be given two weeks to review it. Please check it carefully, and let us know if any text is missing or substantially altered. (Major alterations by the editor will usually be discussed with the author, so we are talking about unexpected changes.)

Another editor pointed out that the last sentence (in parentheses) describes a procedure that occurs *before* the galley copy is sent. Not very chronological—or *logical*! Here's what I changed it to:

> If any major revisions need to be done at the editing stage, the editor will contact you to discuss the changes. Then, as we get near the end of our editing, typesetting, and proofreading process, we will send you a galley copy of the typeset manuscript to review.

As you can see, once I had changed the order around chronologically, it became clear that there was no need to mention the two-week deadline at this point, or to insult their intelligence by telling them how to review the galley ("let us know if any text is missing" and so on). Chronological order often makes the message clearer by making extraneous information more obvious.

When I suggest you work on the logical flow of your writing, I am not talking about deep, scholarly thinking or ivory-tower meditations, performed by dark-robed professorial types. All I mean is following the pattern of the way people think.

Actually, *logic* does not always describe the way people think, because people think illogically all the time. Logic is probably best defined as the way people think *together*—the commonly accepted, universal language of the mind. If I think and express myself to you logically, you will be able to follow my train of thought. But if I think and express myself illogically, it's anyone's guess if you can follow my train of thought, because the train has leaped the tracks and is roaming the countryside!

If I appear to be going overboard to define and defend logic, it is because some Christians seem to think it's not spiritual. (Are they implying that *God* is not logical?) While it is true that many things in the spiritual realm do not conform to our narrow, limited human minds, that is hardly a reason to throw out logical thinking altogether. It's about the same as saying that I cannot write anything with the authority and inspiration of the Bible, so I won't bother writing anything at all.

In fiction you can expect the reader to hold a certain "suspension of disbelief"—to stay in a pretend-mode and accept what would be confusing or implausible in real life. (Isn't it amazing, for instance, that a pair of glasses is the only disguise Clark Kent needs to keep Lois Lane from recognizing he's Superman?) In nonfiction, you can't depend on that if you want to keep the reader with you. You must assume that every word you write will be questioned. Ya follow me?

Murphy's Law Applied to Writing

One of the most important things I learned about writing came about when I was working as an editor of instructional manuals for a heavy equipment manufacturer. And it relates to the story behind "Murphy's Law."

I am not talking about the popular bit of cynicism referred to as Murphy's Law—"If anything can go wrong, it will." I am talking about a more practical and universal truth—and yes, there was a real man behind it named Murphy.

In 1949, while testing an experimental rocket sled, the engineers on the project discovered that every one of the sensors used on the sled had been wired backwards by an assistant—inspiring this put-down by one of the engineers, Edward Murphy: "If there is any way to do it wrong, he will." [3]

To phrase this in more general terms (and let Murphy's much-maligned assistant off the hook), "If there is a wrong way to do something, someone will discover it." In other words, it's hard to make something foolproof, because fools are so ingenious!

As writers of technical manuals, my colleagues and I immediately saw the importance of this principle. If people are prone to doing things the wrong way, we had better make sure we anticipate all the possible mistakes someone might make, and warn them in the instructions. To discover such mistakes, we often took a stroll down to the shop floor and watched the workers put together the equipment. It was always a learning experience.

One time we watched a worker with a huge rubber mallet driving a large steel pulley onto a shaft, which was then covered by a sheet-metal cowling. The worker was banging away on the pulley, trying to drive it onto the shaft. He was making an awful racket, and so the foreman walked over and asked what was going on.

"Well, boss, I had the hardest time getting this pulley onto the shaft, but I finally did it."

"You idiot!" the foreman replied. (Actually, he said something else, but this is a Christian book.) "That shaft is tapered to match the tapered hole in the center of the pulley. The reason you had so much trouble is because you put it on *backwards*. Now put the cowling over that pulley before anybody sees it!"

Looking over his shoulder, the foreman saw us and a twinge of guilt crossed his face, but he quickly decided that we were no threat. (Technical writers had no authority whatsoever in the company, so we were good at playing dumb.) We hurried back to the office and made a note to the assembly manual writer: "Warn reader not to put pulley on backwards."

By now you're probably asking how this principle applies to Christian writing. It is simply this: if there is any way to misunderstand what you are writing, someone in your audience *will* misunderstand it. If it can be misinterpreted, it will be, so try to anticipate where your reader might get confused, and *clarify* it, *amplify* it, or *simplify* it. Epictetus, the ancient Greek orator and Stoic philosopher, put it this way: "Do not write so that you can be understood, write so that you cannot be misunderstood."

The way to avoid misinterpretation, then, is to remember two things:

1.   Read and *reread* what you've written, and ask yourself if there is any way someone could misinterpret it. This is why I suggested setting your rough draft aside for a few days before you review it. It is an excellent and practical way to look at your words as if you are seeing them for the first time. I often find that I think I'm making sense, but then as I look over the material a couple of days later, I discover sentences and phrases that only made sense when my creative juices were flowing (a half-crazed mental condition that is not prone to clear and lucid thinking).

2. Another way to discover passages that could be misunderstood is to show the draft to a few other people. If there's anything confusing or ambiguous there, they'll find it, trust me. (My wife found a couple of rough spots in this very chapter, in fact!) This is probably the best argument for joining a critique group.

If you follow these practices, you'll discover that your manuscript begins to shine with clarity. But don't thank me—the credit goes to two great philosophers, Epictetus and Edward Murphy.

Once you've got those revisions done, you're on the home stretch. But before you send off that manuscript, there's one more step: fine-tuning.

REVISION TIP #1:

Take note of particular phrases that sound vaguely familiar, and do a global search for them in the entire manuscript. If such phrases turn up more than three or four times, remove most of them. If a phrase is a bona fide cliché, strike it out! (Okay, I confess. I love clichés and although my editor struck most of them, she allowed me to keep a couple of my favorites in this manuscript.)

REVISION TIP #2:

Expanding the length of a first draft involves *adding content*, not merely reiterating points that have already been made. Look for terms that need to be defined, points that need to be explained, and instructions that need to be broken down into steps.

REVISION TIP #3:

Two of the most overused words in the English language are *which* and *that*. Go on a "which" hunt! Rethink every instance of "that." Not every usage of *which* and *that* is unnecessary, but a great many are.

CHAPTER **8**

FINE-TUNING THE MANUSCRIPT

I love being a writer. What I can't stand is the paperwork.

— Peter De Vries

If we lived in an ideal world, you would finish the revisions to your manuscript just about the time that a contract for the book arrived in the mail. You would sign the contract, pack up your manuscript, and send it off to the publisher, as you sit back and wait for fame and fortune to smile upon you.

Don't get too comfortable.

In the real world, and especially if you're a first-time author, you may find that the publisher does not intend to sign on the dotted line without getting a good look at a complete manuscript. Before you send it off, however, there are a number of final tweaks you can make to the manuscript that will save you and your publisher a lot of headaches—little niceties that can make or break a decision to offer a contract. Even if you already have a contract, taking care of these nasty little details will make you the kind of author that a publisher wants to publish again—and there's no time like the present to begin selling your publisher on your next book!

So, what little details am I talking about? Read on:

1. Credit Lines

Many books are delayed because of incomplete credit lines. One thing that drives me crazy is getting halfway through editing a book and finding an extensive quote without a credit line. And then when I contact the author about it, the most typical response is, "Oh, I read that *somewhere.*" This is not the way to win friends and influence people!

If you remember, I told you when we were discussing research to keep notes of where you find material (author, title, publisher, date, page number). If you've been faithful in doing this, the credit issue should be no problem. (If you *haven't* kept notes—well, you have some work to do.) For all quoted material, simply provide an endnote or footnote with all the appropriate information (which can be found on the copyright page of the source book). It should be in this format: author's name, title of the book (in italics), city, publisher and date of publication (in parentheses), and page number. In other words, it looks like this:

> David Fessenden, *How I Lost Five Hundred Pounds by Eating Insects* (Fresno, CA: Heartburn Books, 1998), pp. 47-48.

(Don't bother looking for that book; I didn't really write one with that title. Besides, it was only three hundred pounds.)

If you quote a magazine or newspaper article, you put the title of the article in quotes instead of italics, put the magazine name in italics, and include the issue date of the magazine instead of the city, publisher, and date:

> David Fessenden, "Eating Insects for Fun and Profit," *Gourmet Today*, May 2000, p. 23.

There are other credit line formats used for quoting someone when interviewing them, or quoting an unpublished letter, etc. But for the most part, unless you are writing an academic book, you need only provide a credit line for published material. The unpublished material can be "credited" in the body of the text. For example, if you interviewed me and wanted to quote me directly, you could say something like this in your book (without needing a credit line):

> Of course, limiting your diet to nothing but insects requires a great deal of self-control. David Fessenden told me recently, "Yes, it's really tough, but I have learned that blah, blah, blah . . ."

If you express the *ideas* of another author, but you don't directly *quote* them, do you need to include a credit line? The answer is yes. For example, in my book on Sunday school teaching, I mention Cynthia Tobias' theory of different learning styles. I haven't quoted her directly—I haven't even discussed her theory in great detail—but just to be fair to her, I have included a credit line. When in doubt, provide a credit line; it can't hurt.

Some authors rebel at all this attention to detail. In fact, one of our authors claimed that no other publisher had ever asked him for credit lines—even though he quoted multiple pages of material from other books! But remember the Golden Rule: how would *you* like to have your book quoted from extensively, with no mention of where it came from? If someone wants to buy your book, they may not be able to find it if they don't know the title and publisher.

If an editor says you have to go back and dig up the information for a credit line, remember that the editor is trying to *protect* you. It's not your *editor's* problem if there is a lawsuit for plagiarism or copyright violation—it's *your* problem. Most contracts stipulate that the *author* is legally responsible to obtain credit lines and permission for any copyrighted material.

2. Permissions

Which brings up the subject of getting permission for all those quotes. This is your job as well, and it's crucial, because it keeps you out of legal trouble. It's also a tough job, because the copyright law is very complex.

Many authors have said to me, "Oh, I don't worry about getting permission for quotes, because the copyright law says you can quote three hundred words without having to ask permission." *This is a myth!*

The copyright law does refer to what it calls "fair use" of material, but please believe me when I say that no word count is used anywhere in the law. Let me refer you to *Kirsch's Handbook of Publishing Law*:

"The folklore of book publishing holds that a quotation of 300 words or less is *always* fair use—but the folklore is simply wrong." [1]

So what "rules" do you use to determine if you need to get permission? Kirsch mentions several things, but it's safe to say that for our purposes, only three rules usually apply—as simple as A, B, C:

A. *Is the material copyrighted, or is it public domain?* The King James Version of the Bible is public domain, for example; I could quote the entire text without having to ask anyone. (Besides, whom would I ask? Everyone who worked on it has been dead for over 300 years!) Even if the author is dead, however, the copyright may still be valid, and you will have to ask the author's publisher and/or estate for permission.

Copyright for most material lasts for the life of the author plus seventy years. If the author of the material you want to quote died over seventy years ago, you can figure it's public domain, and you can freely use it without asking anyone. If you don't know when the author died, but you know the material has been in print for over a century, it is probably public domain as well, but be careful. If someone has revised an old book—rephrased it into modern English, for example—the revised version is probably copyrighted. If someone has translated an old text from some other language into English, the English text is probably copyrighted. When in doubt, ask permission.

B. *How much of the original material is used, in comparison to the whole thing?* If you quote fifty words from a five hundred-word article, you had better get permission—that's *10 percent* of the material! But if you quote fifty words from a five hundred-page book, most likely you wouldn't bother. Poems and songs, by their nature, are quite restrictive; some poetry consists of only a few dozen words, so even a short phrase could be considered a substantial portion of the piece.

At this point in my writing workshops, someone usually stands up and shouts, "What a bunch of garbage!" (Well, maybe they're not that dramatic about it, but you get the idea.) "Why must I get permission for a poem or a song," they ask, "when I can find the full text of it on the Internet?" The answer is that life isn't fair. Websites and bloggers regularly violate copyright laws, and they rarely seem to be sued, apparently because it's hard to pin down; with a few keystrokes, they can remove the evidence. But as Christians, we should obey the law and respect the rights of fellow authors, regardless of what others do. Remember what your mother used to say: "Would you jump off a cliff if everyone else was doing it?"

C. *How will your quoting of the material affect the market for the material?* If you spend an entire chapter in your book quoting and paraphrasing all the main points of another book, the reader could legitimately say, "I know the gist of that other book, so why should I buy it?" You have probably crossed the line and harmed the sales of that book, even though you didn't directly quote much of it; so you better ask for permission—and in a case like that, you may get charged to use the quote, or permission may even be refused! (See how this also relates to rule B above?) On the positive side, if you quote a short passage of a book, it may *increase* sales of the other book—it's good advertising—and they would probably give you permission; in fact, you probably don't even need to ask.

Is there a simple rule of thumb to determine whether you should get permission for a quote? No, there isn't, unless you want to call "When in doubt, ask" a rule of thumb. I advise authors to avoid quoting short pieces such as poetry (one author I know quoted *one verse* of a popular song and had to pay three hundred dollars for it!), to ask permission for any quote from a magazine, and to get permission for anything from a good-sized book that is more than a sentence or two. But—and this is a big but—don't take my suggestions as any kind of legal advice, because I'm not an attorney. If you want to know more, check out *Kirsch's Handbook of Publishing Law*, or look at the fourth chapter of *The Chicago Manual of Style*.[2]

I have provided you with a sample permission letter to use when you write a publisher (see Appendix B). If you are writing for permission before you have a contract with a publisher (and you don't know all the details of price, format, etc.), simply give the name of your book and explain that you are seeking a publisher. Writing even before you have a contract is a good idea. Who knows? The title of the book may spark the interest of the publisher from whom you are asking permission. Don't hold your breath, but it has happened before.

Another good reason to write before you have a contract is that publishers may be more inclined to give permission for free if you don't have a contract yet. If you have a contract, the copyright owner knows you're under a publishing deadline, and they are in a better bargaining position. Of course, you probably still have time to bargain or even remove a quote if you have a contract. What's bad is when, very late in the editorial process, the editor finds a long quote that really needs permission. Then the copyright owner can charge almost any price, because it's getting too late to remove the quote and make any necessary revisions in the manuscript. And if they ask for a stiff payment, *you* will pay it, not your publisher!

3. Bible Translations

Another detail that can cause problems later is the use of multiple Bible translations. My suggestion is to use one translation and, with few exceptions, stick to it. The editor checks the wording of every Bible verse you use, and if you use a half dozen different translations, it becomes time-consuming—especially if you do not identify the translations you are using, and the editor has to figure it out.

Another good reason to stick with one translation is that it's another way to make sure you are using Scripture correctly. If I have to look at a dozen translations before I can find wording that appears to support my opinion, maybe my opinion is not all that biblical. So, for the most part, use one translation you are comfortable with, and make note of that at the beginning of your manuscript—"Unless otherwise noted, all Scripture is in the New International Version." If you quote from any other translation, put the initials of the translation (such as KJV, NIV, NASB, and the rest of the "alphabet soup" of today's translations) with the reference in parentheses after the verse—"Jesus wept" (John 11:35 KJV). You should also provide a list of the translations you used, since the publisher needs to include a copyright notice for each translation on the copyright page (one more reason to avoid the use of too many translations).

When the text of a Scripture quote is three lines or less in your manuscript (less than five or six lines when typeset), keep it in quotes, and put the reference in parentheses *outside* the quotes, as above. If the quotation exceeds three lines of manuscript text, you should indent the Scripture passage, remove the quotation marks, and put the reference in parentheses *after* the period:

> Then Asa called to the LORD his God and said, "LORD, there is no one besides You to help in the battle between the powerful and those who have no strength; so help us, O LORD our God, for we trust in You, and in Your name have come against this multitude. O LORD, You are our God; let not man prevail against You. (2 Chronicles 14:11 NASB)

How much of a Bible translation can you use? The King James is public domain—use as much of it as you want; most other translations in use today are copyrighted, but the publishers recognize the need to allow free use of the Bible. Zondervan, for example, which controls the copyright of the NIV, allows you to quote up to five hundred verses, as long as a complete book of the Bible is not quoted and as long as the quotes do not exceed 25 percent of the volume of your book. Other Bible publishers have similar restrictions.

Copyright restrictions on translations should not be a problem for you unless you are writing a verse-by-verse commentary of a book—then you should write and ask permission. Since it's completely understandable that you would quote all the verses of a book of the Bible in a verse-by-verse commentary, they'll probably grant permission without any trouble. But be sure to ask.

4. Style

Spelling, punctuation, capitalization—all are part of what is called *style.* Follow a standard style manual, such as *The Chicago Manual of Style, A Christian Writer's Manual of Style,*[3] or *The Little Style Guide to Great Christian Writing and Publishing.*[4] If necessary (and it probably *is* necessary), get someone else to proofread your manuscript for you.

In a book that uses many names, such as a history or biography, make sure they are all spelled right. When I see someone refer to "C.S. Louis," or when they mention someone several times and spell the person's name *three different ways* in the same chapter (I'm not exaggerating; this actually happened in a manuscript I reviewed), I question the author's ability to get facts straight. If you can't get the details right, where else have you failed to do your homework? Jesus even said that if you can't be faithful in little things, how can you be trusted with big things (Luke 16:10)?

5. Endorsements

Do you know any people who are articulate and in a position of leadership? Perhaps you can ask them for an endorsement. It doesn't hurt if they are famous, but it's enough if they have positions of importance, preferably a position that relates to the topic.

Don't make any guarantees, such as, "I'll put your quote on the back cover." That's not your decision to make. Simply ask the person to review your manuscript (or sometimes, just your proposal and a couple chapters) and tell you what they think. Alert them that any positive statements may be used in the promotion of the book.

Endorsements can be obtained at any point where you have enough of the book for someone to review. I shared my proposal and a couple of chapters of my Sunday school teaching book with several Christian educators and received some good comments—which I then put into the revised version of the proposal.

6. Format for Submission

This depends on whether you are submitting the book *before* or *after* receiving a contract. If it's *before*, most publishers want an electronic file that they can print out a hard copy from—double-spaced, with page numbers, your name and contact information on each page, etc. Check with your publisher. If it's *after*, the publisher may want *two* versions of the electronic file: one suitable for printing out a hard copy, and one for editing. The editing version should *not* have all that formatting; it should simply be raw text that the editor can manipulate and the typesetter can format. But some publishers don't really require an editing copy, so check with your publisher. The most important thing to avoid, as my own editor on this book said, is "fancy-schmancy formatting. Stick to a 12-point, serif font (usually Times New Roman), and don't do cutesy things with the chapter titles, subtitles, etc."

The Bells and Whistles

Finalizing the manuscript is also the point at which you may want to add additional features to your book, such as subheads, sidebars, and study questions.

1. Subheads: Adding subheads to your chapters probably seems easier than it is. Just throw in a title occasionally, right? Actually, good subheads in the right places in your text can be a tremendous aid to the reader. They often serve as a signal to your audience that you are about to make an abrupt transition that would be entirely ineffective if done any other way. Subheads can also help the reader to follow a series of points you want to make, and keep the points integrated, even if each point is separated by multiple pages of explanatory text.

With your outline at hand, take a closer look at the flow of the text in each chapter. You may be surprised just how much more understandable a long chapter can be with the judicious use of subheads. Just don't overdo it; too many subheads (occurring more frequently, on the average, than one major one every two or three pages), or subheads in the wrong place, and they lose their effectiveness.

Also try to avoid subheads that overtly emphasize the structure of the chapter, such as subheads with Roman numerals, followed by sub-subheads in capital letters, followed by sub-sub-subheads—well, you get the idea. Such a stiff structure tends to be hard to follow and overly academic, to the point of being pedantic. Even if you are writing an academic book, this kind of complex structuralism is rather outmoded, even in scholarly circles.

2. Sidebars: Let's imagine you get a phone call from an editor at a publishing house. They like your manuscript, but they are wondering if you could provide one or two sidebars in each chapter. What do you do?

First, you may need to know what a sidebar is. It is like a mini-article containing related information that enhances the value of the main text. These little ditties are usually printed alongside the main text (hence the name), and are intended to draw the reader into the topic. It may be extra work, but be happy if an editor asks for a sidebar; it's an indication that they are taking your material very seriously.

I have included a sidebar on the next page to show you what they look like. And, of course, the sidebar has additional useful information.

So how do you come up with a sidebar? Go back to your original notes when you were brainstorming. Maybe there were ideas or even completed text that you didn't include in a chapter because there wasn't room. Think about your topic from a different perspective; find a tangential concept. If the chapter topic is a virtue, find its opposite—either a different virtue that offsets it, or its corresponding vice. For instance, take humility; its opposing vice would be pride, of course,

> **Submitting Sidebars with Your Manuscript**
> One of the simplest methods of submitting sidebars with your manuscript is to put the full text in the body of the manuscript, indented, at the location you want it to appear, with "begin" and "end" instructions in brackets on separate lines before and after, like this:
>   [BEGIN SIDEBAR]
>   (full text of sidebar)
>   [END SIDEBAR]
> Of course, when your book is accepted for publication, your publisher may prefer that sidebars be submitted in a separate file, or in some other way. Check with your editor.

but its "opposite" virtue might be boldness. Write a short paragraph on how you can be humble and bold at the same time. Or talk about the subtle temptation of pride.

Or, if your chapter is about a spiritual concept, follow it up with a sidebar that shows a practical application of this truth. A chapter on the need for reconciliation when you have offended your brother could be accompanied by a sidebar on how to write a letter of apology. Or, a practical chapter could be accompanied by something more reflective, such as the biblical basis behind it. A chapter on practical tips for sharing your faith, for instance, might have a sidebar that comments on the verse, "He who wins souls is wise" (Prov. 11:30).

Sometimes an anecdote, illustration, or principle that you were unable to find a place for in your chapter can be reworked into a stand-alone sidebar. Another possible sidebar is a quote or group of quotes on the topic from well-known people.

Compiling a list can make a good sidebar—perhaps something like, "You know that [topic] is a problem if . . ." followed by a list of statements. Quizzes are also good—"Are you [topic]?" or, "Do you have [topic]?" followed by a list of professional-sounding "diagnostic" questions. These don't have to be deathly serious; you can even make them humorous, as long as you don't trivialize the topic.

With this in mind, let's say you are writing a chapter for husbands about the importance of praying for their wives. What do you think of the following tongue-in-cheek quiz?

Are You a Good Husband?

1. I wash the dishes or make dinner without being asked.

2. I leave the toilet seat down.

3. My kids know who I am, and never ask me, "What are *you* doing here?"

4. I regularly pray with my wife.

Score one point for a yes to questions 1-3, and 100 points for question number 4. Any score below 100 is unacceptable.

Is this a good sidebar? Well, probably not. It's too cutesy for most editors, and doesn't really provide practical information. So a better alternative might be a list of practical ways that a husband can remind himself to pray with his wife. That would be truly useful.

How do you submit sidebars? One way is to write the sidebar into the appropriate spot in the text as a separate paragraph, and putting [Begin Sidebar] before and [End Sidebar] after. Another way is to submit the sidebars as separate files with the manuscript, so the typesetter can insert them where appropriate. Ask your publisher which way they prefer. *Do not* put sidebars into separate text boxes on the page, because the text in text boxes is often lost in conversion to the typesetting program.

Sidebars can make a book more attractive to a publisher—and to readers. It would be good to get into the habit of writing one or two sidebars for every chapter.

3. Study Questions: Socrates was considered one of the world's greatest teachers, all because he took the time to ask questions. You can make your nonfiction book more publishable by following the same teaching method.

One of the more common little extras that publishers look for when considering a nonfiction book is a set of questions designed to spur group discussion or personal reflection at the end of each chapter. Obviously, no publisher will give you a contract on a book just because it has questions at the end of the chapters, but including such details is a big plus. I know that because a publisher will sometimes pay an outside writer to produce end-of-chapter questions for the new edition of a book they have previously published.

If you want to try your hand at writing study questions, here are a few tips to make your life easier:

- Start by dividing the chapters into logical sections, and then doing one question for each section. It is easier to come up with a question pertaining to a small section of the chapter than to write a half dozen questions that relate to the entire message of the chapter. (If you've already written subheads for the chapter, they are often a good clue as to where the logical divisions are in a chapter.)

- In coming up with questions, look through the chapter for places where you did something different for the sake of emphasis: italicized statements, indented text, rhetorical questions, charts, or diagrams. These zero in on the main points, and your study question should do so as well. It also is worth your while to look up and read the context of any Scripture references in the text. One of the best kinds of questions you can write is one that asks the reader to draw a concept out of a particular passage in the Bible.

- As for the actual content of the questions, it all depends on whether you intend to write questions for group discussion or for personal study. (Some publishers will ask for both, which at the very least doubles your work.) Write personal questions to make the reader think and reflect on what they have read in the chapter. They usually should not be simplistic or obvious, but also should not be so complex or esoteric that the reader cannot answer them. Good reflection questions ask the reader to cull his or her memory for experiences, facts, opinions, and so on. They spur a reader to evaluate the information in the chapter.

- Group discussion questions are much the same as personal study questions, but they need to be less, well, *personal*—in the sense that you are not asking members of the group to share their deepest, darkest secrets with the rest of the group. They can, however, seek an opinion from the group members. If a question brings out honest differences of opinion, all the better.

- When it comes to Scripture, though, it is best to avoid the "What does this passage mean to you?" type of question. Though it is commonly used in some Bible studies, it is dangerous, because it invites the reader to be very subjective in the interpretation of God's Word. You can ask an occasional question that calls for the reader's personal response to a passage, such as, "How would you have reacted if you had been in Peter's shoes?"

- You probably have guessed by now that I recommend open-ended questions (those that require more than a yes, no, or other one-word response). But it can be very effective to ask a question that seeks a short, simple answer, and then follow it up with another question that delves into what is behind the answer to the first question. For example, you may ask, "Do you have trouble maintaining a regular habit of prayer?" and follow it up with, "What changes in your life might improve your prayer time?"

- Finally, avoid what I call "altar call" questions—the kind that a preacher makes just before he asks his audience to "walk the sawdust trail." You know what I mean: the kind of question that presses for an immediate response, such as, "Will you resolve to love God more fully?" The only thing wrong with this is that it doesn't invite the reader to deep reflection. Better to ask a question like, "If you resolved to love God more fully, what changes would it make in your life?"

- If you feel driven to press the reader to "resolve to love God more fully," or respond in some other specific way, don't cloak it in an awkwardly worded question. State outright what you want them to do: "Take a moment now to pray and ask God to help you love Him more fully." These types of statements can be a good way to conclude a series of provocative study questions.

The job of writing end-of-chapter study questions for your book is not an easy one. But it can be one of the most helpful writing projects you've ever done, because good questions cause your readers to really get into the take-away of the book, which means they really learn something. Move over, Socrates!

Ready to Go?

If you've followed the instructions in this chapter you should have a finalized manuscript, ready for an editor to look at. (I've even included a bonus for you. See Appendix A for a "Checklist for Revision and Finalizing of Manuscript.")

Now for the final two acts in this drama: submission and contracting.

FINE-TUNING TIP #1:

Have you spell-checked your manuscript? It may seem rather obvious, but many submitted manuscripts obviously do not go through this step.

FINE-TUNING TIP #2:

Subheads have a function that is often unrecognized: you can make a distinct change of subject in the middle of a chapter with a subhead, and avoid awkward or artificial transitions.

FINE-TUNING TIP #3:

Ask your publisher about discussion/study questions as early in the negotiations as possible. If your publisher doesn't want questions at the end of chapters, you won't waste your time, and if your publisher does want questions, you won't be doing them at the last minute!

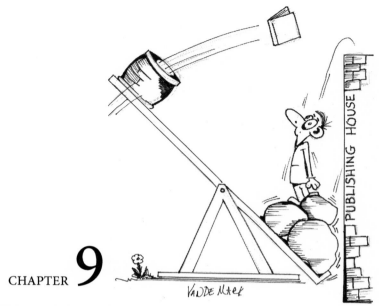

CHAPTER **9**

VANDE MAEK

LANDING THE CONTRACT

The writer writes in order to teach himself, to understand himself, to satisfy himself; the publishing of his ideas, though it brings gratification, is a curious anticlimax.

— Alfred Kazin, *Think*, February 1963

While I wouldn't go so far as to call getting published a "curious anticlimax," I can certainly understand what Alfred Kazin is getting at. It can be very satisfying to get your ideas down on paper, to shape them into a unified, attractive package, and to see a final product that in some ways exceeds even your own expectations. And now I'm raining on your parade by telling you that there's still *more* work to do!

That is why pitching the manuscript to publishers is the weakest point in the process for many authors—including myself, I must confess. It tends to be the part of the process that I try to find shortcuts for—and I've regretted it many times.

If you have produced a good proposal, however, and have gotten some feedback on it so that you have revised and sharpened the presentation, you are halfway home. After finishing the final version of your manuscript, you may be too tired to give a sparkling sales pitch—but your proposal isn't! The proposal will do the heavy lifting for you; all you have to do is get it in front of editors.

Easier said than done, you say? Not at all! Simply follow this battle plan as soon as you have a workable version of the proposal:

1. Prepare a Query Letter to Send to Several Publishers

This is similar to a cover letter, in that you want to present in a few paragraphs the best parts of your proposal. Remember what we said about the cover letter:

First Paragraph: Hook them with a problem, a story, a question. Make sure it's a good one. If it's a problem, it needs to be important, with universal appeal. If it's a story, it has to be a grabber. If it's a question, it has to be compelling. *Don't* use a question that begins with, "Did you know that . . . ?" Some editors are likely to respond, "No, I didn't know that, and I don't care." And into the wastebasket it goes!

Some authors use the first paragraph of their first chapter for the hook. That can work very well sometimes—and if it doesn't work, you should ask yourself why. If that first paragraph doesn't grab the editor in a query letter, maybe it's not the best way to begin the first chapter, either.

Second Paragraph: An abbreviated version of the premise statement, and two or three of your most compelling arguments from the proposal.

Third Paragraph: Details about length and format. Do you envision it as a soft-cover trade book, a mass-market, a hardcover, a "gift" book? Take your choice, but recognize that the vast majority of books published today are soft-cover trade format. Also tell them how soon you can have the manuscript ready (if it is not yet completed), followed by "I look forward to hearing from you."

2. Check a Market Guide and Guidelines for Several Publishers

Send a query simultaneously to those who specifically say they accept queries. Simultaneous queries are not the same as simultaneous submissions. It would not be unusual to send to a dozen publishers, but make sure you customize the letter for each one—no "Dear Publisher" generic letters. Include a self-addressed, stamped postcard for the publisher to say yes or no, and/or (as most guidelines now say) include your e-mail address.

If the publisher allows an e-mail query, use the same format as above for your letter; don't be cutesy with smiley faces and abbreviations like "LOL" or "ROTFL"; maintain the formality of a business letter, even if it is by e-mail.

3. Send a Proposal to All Who Respond Positively

At this point, you need to check if they will accept simultaneous submissions of proposals. When some publishers say "no simultaneous submissions," they mean complete manuscripts only; others mean proposals as well. If you can, send it to multiple publishers. The cover letter should be similar to the query letter, only you begin by acknowledging that they asked for the proposal: "Thank you for giving me the opportunity to show you my proposal . . ." Send the full manuscript if the publisher asks for it and you have it completed. If you have to send a proposal or manuscript to a single publisher, make sure you emphasize that fact in your cover letter: "This submission is being sent to you *exclusively*..."

Many publishers will accept submissions of proposals and manuscripts by attached file to an e-mail. If your publisher allows this, be sure you are not making more work for the editor. Unfortunately, many authors seem to make the process unnecessarily complicated. One editor recently told me that he had just received a proposal and three sample chapters from an author—in no less than *eight* separate attached files! There is no reason why the material could not have been sent as a single file.

4. Take Several Copies of the Proposal to Writers' Conferences

Show it around and get some feedback—but don't feel you have to "sell" yourself or your book. Let your proposal do the selling job— you're just along for the ride. Editors and agents spend much of their time at conferences getting a hard sell from over-eager authors. If they see that you are *not* trying to push your manuscript but simply want some feedback on your proposal, it will be a nice change of pace for them. Sometimes it's a good idea to show it to editors and agents who may *not* deal with manuscripts in your genre. When they don't feel pressured to acquire your book, they can relax and look at the proposal objectively, and you'll usually get some good advice. Of course, I hope that you will also meet some editors and agents who *do* deal with your kind of manuscript—but don't let that change your low-key approach. (I'll get into more detail about editorial appointments later.)

Don't forget that editors and agents talk to each other, too. Many times I've reviewed a proposal at a writers' conference that was great but did not fit our editorial needs (sorry if that sounds too much like a rejection letter!), so I recommended it to another editor or agent, who asked the author for it. It really feels good to have an editor ask *you* for a look at your proposal!

You might also be wrong about what a particular publishing house or agency is looking for. Publishers try to be clear and specific about the kind of material they are seeking, but most acquisition editors are open to the unexpected and distinctive book idea that does not fit neatly into their categories. At a recent conference I handed the proposal for this book to an editor at Sonfire Media, expecting nothing more than some feedback. Was I ever surprised when they sent me a contract! (And the other proposal I sent Sonfire, which I thought was a perfect fit for them, was rejected. Go figure.)

5. Based on the Feedback You Receive, Revamp the Proposal as Needed

If an evaluation—even a rejection—includes some positive comments, add them (only the *positive* comments, please!) to the revised proposal. Probably the simplest way to do this is to put a subhead such as "reader comments" and quote the editors verbatim, with their names and job titles. There's no need to say, "Well, it was rejected, but the editor really liked it, etc., etc."

The feedback you get from rejections should motivate you to go back to revision—maybe even back to brainstorming, researching, and outlining—and make the extra tweaks that will result in a better book. (If you thought that being in the last stage of the writing cycle meant you had finished the previous steps, you haven't been listening!)

Perhaps you've had your book turned down, but no one is giving you suggestions for improvement. That's not surprising if you submitted it by postal mail or e-mail. Editors and agents are swamped with submissions, and there is never enough time to give authors the feedback they deserve. Of course, another reason you may not be getting suggestions for improvement is that the book is in good shape. Many books are rejected simply because the publishing house has all the books it can possibly handle at the moment.

6. Keep Good Records

Mark down where and when you sent the query, proposal, or manuscript, and when you got a response. It's easier to be patient while you wait for a response if you know exactly when you sent your submission. And it prevents duplication of effort. (It can be embarrassing to discover that you just sent your proposal to the same editor who sent you a rejection the previous week.)

Knowing who said what about your manuscript can be very useful if you meet that editor or agent at a writers' conference. You can remind the editor about your book and thank them for any encouraging words they had to share when they turned it down. A friend of mine had just such a conversation with an editor at a recent conference, and he decided to take a second look at the book he had rejected.

7. Finally, Don't Be Discouraged

Rejections are part of the process. I know that doesn't make them hurt any less. Veteran authors are rejected, too, and it still hurts. The only solution is to develop a thick hide as you maintain a teachable heart—a tough balance, but you can do it. Pray over every rejection, and accept it as God's will. If you're really having a bad day, *reread* the positive comments and endorsements in your proposal. They will remind you why you wrote the book in the first place, and inspire you to send out your proposal again.

It may take several rounds, several revisions, and several years to find a home for your manuscript. Nobody said it would be easy!

Your Fifteen Minutes of Fame

Your first writer's conference may yield a few surprises—not the least of which may be the opportunity to have a one-on-one appointment with a real, live editor or agent. It can be intimidating, but if you prepare well, everything should work out fine. So, aside from hyperventilating, how do you prepare for this?

First, get the author guidelines for the publishing house or agency the person represents, and review them. Also check out the person's biographical information, and/or talk to a few people who know the person. Choose either someone who works with the kind of material you are writing, or who seems knowledgeable about the market.

Which leads to the next question: what is your reason for making the appointment? Be sure to make that clear at the very beginning of your meeting. Pitching a completed manuscript is only *one* reason to make an appointment. You may want to have an evaluation of your book proposal. You may want to ask what the agency or publishing house is looking for in new authors. You may even want to use an appointment to brainstorm your next book idea—which is fine, as long as you're realistic about it. An editor may be able to help you focus your idea, but don't expect them to outline it for you.

Editorial Appointments: What to Expect

1. **You should get an honest, even perhaps a blunt, critique.** Remember that you may be the umpteenth person the editor or agent has seen today, and diplomacy can wear a bit thin after a while. I find that if you steel yourself emotionally for the worst, it's never that bad—you might even be pleasantly surprised!

2. **Expect encouragement.** An agent or editor should never criticize your work without giving you some encouragement and a few hints on how to make it better. If you get nothing but negative feedback and no real help, shake the dust from your feet and go to the next appointment. Don't waste your energy on that negative

person—they'll never make it in this business, anyway. I doubt that you'll run into many people like that. Most editors and agents I know are very hesitant to discourage a new author, especially because new authors can surprise you. Some authors I thought were hopeless are now veteran pros. I am continually amazed at what God can do in a yielded life, given enough time.

3. **Expect suggestions for improvement.** You will usually get some very good advice, along with a little bad advice as well; no editor or agent is perfect. How do you tell if the advice is valid or not? The majority rules. If you meet with three different people and two or even all three say the same thing, you probably should listen. More often than not, however, you won't need to verify the advice; you will *know* it is right. Editors and agents have an uncanny ability to zero in on the very thing you knew—but didn't want to admit—was wrong with your proposal or manuscript.

    Ouch, that hurts! But in a way, it shows you are improving as a writer; you've gotten past the point of being oblivious to the weaknesses in your manuscript. I sometimes struggle with a writing project, frustrated that it isn't working right. Then an editor or agent looks at it, makes three or four words of critique, and I say, "Of course! Why didn't I see that?"

4. **Expect to hear some obscure writing jargon or vague comments.** We editors and agents are supposed to be experts at communicating, but we all fall short once in a while. So don't be afraid to ask what a "lead" is, or what they mean by a "flowery style" or the "take-away." If an editor or agent tells you

your writing is wordy, for example, ask him or her to show you a specific paragraph and how it might be shortened.

Editorial Appointments: What Not to Expect

1. **Don't expect to be laughed at.** (Now be honest: isn't that your secret fear?) The editor or agent will take you seriously. And if you have prepared well, you will be taken even more seriously. Remember that the editor or agent is not there for fun. He or she is looking (often desperately) for manuscripts to publish or peddle to publishers. Many editors I know are also writers, so they know what it's like to be in your shoes.

2. **Don't expect an editor to offer you a contract for the book or an agent to commit to take you on as a client.** Most editors do not (and for that matter, *cannot*) commit to publishing a book without bringing others in the publishing house into the decision. And if an agent takes you on too eagerly, it may be a red flag (we will take a closer look at agents in a moment). The best you can hope for is that the editor or agent takes a copy of your proposal home for further review. (A word to the wise: bring several copies of your proposal with you to the conference.)

3. **Don't expect to learn secrets that will magically transform you into a great writer.** There's not enough time in an appointment for that. (Besides, if I knew some great secret like that, I'd put it in *this* book and make a million dollars!) But you may be able to pick up a few tips that, combined with time and diligence, can improve your writing.

A typical appointment is about fifteen minutes. Try to present yourself and your proposal (or writing question, or book idea) in the first three minutes. The editor or agent may ask a few questions, make a few comments, and spend some time reading your material. *Don't talk* while the person is reading. (The temptation is overwhelming, I know!)

If all goes well, you have about five minutes to get a critique, encouragement, and advice. Doesn't sound like enough time? It's not! Editors and writers often say how frustrating it can be. But sometimes you continue a conversation with an editor over a meal or in the hallway between sessions of the conference. Some of the best advice I've gotten came through a post-appointment conversation.

Checklist for Editorial Appointments

1. Pray about the meeting. (How often we all forget to do that!) Pray for yourself and the editor or agent.

2. Study the submission guidelines for the agency or publishing house ahead of time. If you don't have the guidelines or a current writer's market guide, look on the company's website.

3. Prepare a hard copy of your book proposal and a sample chapter or partial chapter to give to the editor or agent. Make sure it is no more than ten pages, because anything over that will not be read—there just isn't enough time. Put your best foot forward: even a draft of a proposal needs to be as polished as possible.

4. Prepare a short (one page) biography of yourself, with accomplishments, education, writing credits—anything that explains your interest in the topic you are writing about and your expertise, if any, in the subject. Include contact information and, if possible, a photo of yourself (faces are often so much easier to remember than names). Make multiple copies so that the agent or editor can keep the material.

5. Bring paper and pen to write down the person's brilliant suggestions. Bring extra paper and pen for the editor, who may forget to bring his or her own (they can be just as scatterbrained as the rest of us!).

6. Come with an open mind, and decide ahead of time that you will not argue or become defensive. And yet, while you need to be open to suggestions for revision, you should have a clear vision of what you want the book to be, and be ready to convey that vision to the editor or agent. If the person misunderstands the intended thrust of your idea, he or she may not give you the correct advice.

7. Afterward, pray about the advice you are given, and ask the Lord to give you wisdom to take the wheat and leave the chaff. Ask for diligence to work on the revisions you need to do.

The Question of Agents

I wish I had a nickel for every time I've been asked a question similar to these:

"I've written a book—should I get an agent?"

"Does your publishing house prefer to work with agents?"

"Does an agented manuscript have a better chance of success at your publishing house?"

Such questions come from authors at all levels of experience. And many are surprised to find that I cannot answer such questions with a simple yes or no. In fact, my short answer to these questions is usually, "It depends on the agent." There are agents that I wouldn't wish upon my worst enemy. And there are other agents who seem to have a golden touch.

The best agents are usually so much in demand that they cannot take on new clients. The worst agents take on as many clients as they can get, and try to sell everything their clients produce, whether good or bad. (I have actually had agents tell me how great a manuscript is, and later admit to me that they haven't read it!)

So when an author looks for an agent, I usually suggest they avoid those who are booked solid (they don't have time for you, so why frustrate yourself?), and avoid those who seem willing to sign you up without a careful, critical look at your material.

By the way, there are some "agents" who charge a fee to read your material; this is not considered a legitimate practice in the publishing industry. Of course, there are agents who also provide editorial services for a fee, and there is nothing wrong with that. But I would be leery of anyone who asks you to pay them for an evaluation.

This, of course, brings up another, more pointed, answer to the question "Should I get an agent?" which is, "It depends on the writer." Can you catch the interest of an agent? Are you a writer who can be a profitable client to an agent?

Of course, it depends on the type of manuscript as well. Agents used to deal almost exclusively with fiction, while many, if not most, nonfiction writers were published without an agent's involvement. Now many agents are taking on nonfiction clients, as well. Is a good agent worth the cost (maybe 15 percent of the royalties) for a Christian nonfiction writer? Probably, especially if the author is prolific (multi-book) and has potential to be popular. Is an agent a *necessity*? Not at this point in time, but the Christian publishing business, as with all of publishing, is going through monumental change, so stay tuned.

Many publishers get most or all of their authors though agent referrals. These publishers depend on agents to weed out the people who can't write and refuse to learn. They also weed out those who can't be bothered to take the time to read the author guidelines (located on almost every publisher's website).

I noted in the first chapter that beginning writers, if they are smart, will hone their skills on magazine articles before they tackle a book-length project. If you followed that advice, then you should have at least a few published samples of your work. These articles can be the key to getting an agent, because most agents aren't interested in working with you unless you have some writing credits.

Is the light beginning to dawn? If you want to get a book-length nonfiction project published, a good agent, while not required, can provide invaluable assistance. How do you get an agent interested? By writing some good articles—which you can get into print through your own submission efforts.

Another facet of the "do I need an agent" question came to mind recently when I received an e-mail from a local author who wanted us to look at his manuscript. I sent him our submission guidelines, but he immediately wrote back to say that he did not have time to follow the "routine way" of submitting a manuscript. He wanted me to come to his office and let him show me what he had to offer.

Do you see the arrogance in this attitude? He wanted to bypass the normal (I should say the only) method of submission because he considered himself too important to do it. (I get phone calls, e-mails, and letters all the time from authors like this, who want to know the "secret shortcut" to being published. Guess what? There isn't one!) This is the type of author who would never attract the interest of an agent, or a publisher for that matter.

The fact that you are reading this book takes you out of that "wannabe" category and into the upper 10 percent of authors—those who put work into their manuscript and are willing to take advice. These authors take the time to find out what types of books a publisher is interested in before submitting. These authors prepare a tightly written proposal that clearly presents their book, and they diligently show it around at writers' conferences. These authors are the ones who get published. Do authors like that need an agent? It wouldn't hurt, but they can probably be published without one.

Planning for Success

You've sent your manuscript off to the publisher, and they have it under consideration. Now begins the l-o-n-g process of waiting. What do you do while you're waiting? You act like someone whose manuscript has already been accepted. "Don't quit your day job," as they say, but do start planning your promotion of the book once it gets published.

Start a website. Start a blog. Go on Facebook. Do whatever it is you do with Twitter. Start telling your friends. Yes, it will be embarrassing if you never get it published, but stop thinking so negatively. I've known of authors who had so much promotion going on their book long before it was accepted that they hit the ground running when it finally was published. Their friends were probably sick of hearing about it, but good friends will put up with a lot. (If you don't believe me, ask *my* friends!)

It can actually be embarrassing *not* to tell others about your book; when they find out, they think you've been hiding your light under a bushel. At a church meeting, my pastor asked me what I had done last weekend. I told him I taught a Sunday school seminar based on my book. "You wrote a book? You teach seminars?" he asked incredulously, loud enough for everyone else in the room to hear. "So how come you haven't done a seminar at *our* church?"

The Publishing Contract

Congratulations! The day has finally arrived. You received that fateful phone call to tell you that your first book is going to be published.

And they're actually going to pay you for it! Now for the bad news: in the mail come two copies of a strangely worded document with an imposing name such as "Publishing Agreement"—and you don't get your money until you sign it.

What do you do? Sign it without reading it at all? Hire a high-priced intellectual-property attorney to look it over? You probably don't want to go in either direction, but there are some definite steps you can take:

1. Consider meeting with a local business attorney.[1] A single conference should provide a realistic evaluation of the basic contract, and point out areas that require careful consideration or further explanation. This consultation will also make you more efficient in completing the remaining steps.

Since a contract for a first-time author should be straightforward for the business attorney, the fees should be reasonable; however, it's always a good idea to discuss costs ahead of time.

2. Evaluate the publisher that is offering you the contract. Do you know other authors who have had a good experience with this company? Have they been in business for a while? Are they well respected? If so, the publisher is likely to offer you a reasonable contract. You shouldn't sign the contract without reading it, but you also shouldn't be suspicious of every single word.

The agreement is probably their first-time author's contract—it may not be a generous offer, but remember that this is your first contract. If the contract is with a small-to-midsized publishing house (and it probably is, because larger publishers are looking for more experienced authors with a proven record of accomplishment), you can expect that the company has more to lose than you do. No publisher can afford to get a reputation for underhanded legal tricks. Word gets around, especially in the smaller Christian publishing community.

3. Do a little research on book contracts. One resource I recommend is *Kirsch's Handbook of Publishing Law*, a surprisingly entertaining read for such a detailed and comprehensive reference work. *Kirsch's Handbook* covers all the clauses of a typical publishing contract in detail. Invest a little time between its pages and you may understand your contract better than your editor. (I understand that Mr. Jonathan Kirsch is planning to update his handbook and merge it with his *Guide to the Book Contract*—I can't wait.)

4. Check the contract for the details you negotiated before you accepted the offer. What? You didn't know there were any details to negotiate? That's not a problem. The details can still be discussed if you haven't signed anything. Some bargaining points include:

- *Royalty advance*: An advance is the amount of royalty the publisher will pay you *in advance* (hence the name). A common rule of thumb for an appropriate advance is the book's anticipated royalties in the first six months. The typical advance on your first book is usually small— the publisher doesn't want to risk too much—but there is usually some room for negotiation. You won't talk them into three times as much as they offer, but a 20-30 percent increase is not unreasonable—and in some cases, you might even ask for more. The worst that can happen is they will turn you down. (In a recent trend, the tough economy has led some publishers to stop offering royalty advances altogether. Please don't shoot the messenger.)

- *Royalty percentage*: A typical royalty rate for a first-time author used to be 10 percent of net sales, but today many publishers pay a little better than that. You can always ask for a higher percentage, but as a first-timer, you are usually not in a great bargaining position. You may be successful, however, if you ask for the standard royalty rate for the first ten thousand books sold, and a higher rate after that. Since most publishers would be thrilled if a first-time author's book sold over ten thousand, they may be willing to accept that. You can also ask for a higher percentage on e-book sales; some publishers offer as much as double the normal royalty.

- *Author's copies*: If they offer you ten copies, ask for twenty-five. It's a small concession for them, and it allows them to feel generous. Besides, you get *fifteen* more copies!

- *Deadline for author to complete manuscript*: If the book is not completed, make sure they are giving you a reasonable deadline. If you just can't get it done on their schedule, counter with a challenging but honest deadline, taking into account that life always throws you a curve or two. Your publisher can usually give you extra time if you need it—but don't push the limits. However, if your proposal states a specific deadline, such as, "I can have the book done within three months of signing a contract," you had better stick to your word!

5. As you review other clauses in the document, you may find them easier to understand and accept if you try to put yourself in the publisher's shoes. One standard clause, for example, allows the publisher to get out of the contract if the author's reputation has been seriously tarnished. Some novice authors take that as a personal insult, or they worry that the publisher will dump them if they get a parking ticket. But this clause is merely to protect the publisher against the unthinkable. If you were a publisher and your author of a book on Christian integrity was convicted of *robbing a bank*, wouldn't you want to get out of the contract?

6. When all else fails, ask your publisher what a particular contract clause means. They should be willing to explain it to you. Don't let them dismiss your questions with "Oh, that's just a standard clause." Tell them, "I'm sure it is, but I would like to be sure that I understand it." No honest publisher will argue with that.

7. Remember, the goal is to reach an evenhanded agreement that benefits both the publisher and the author. A contract weighted in either direction will create more problems than it solves.

8. And you most certainly should pray about the contract offer! God gives wisdom to those who ask (James 1:5).

A Final Word

We've reached the end of this book, but your work—aren't you getting tired of hearing me say this?—is just beginning. Now you have before you the job of publicizing and promoting your book, of which entire volumes could be written—and actually, they have been. I encourage you to read and learn as much as you can about publicity and promotion, and work with your publisher to get the word out about your book. Effort early in the process can reap great rewards.

Perhaps you are also ready to start working on your next book. I hope you have found the eight-step process helpful, and are ready to start back at the brainstorming stage—this time with a little more experience under your belt. Go forth as a scribe of the Kingdom, who "brings out of his storeroom new treasures as well as old" (Matthew 13:52). May the Lord bless your literary efforts and use them for His glory!

CONTRACT TIP #1:

Sometimes an indirect contact will help you connect with an agent or publisher. An author friend may be able to introduce you to a great agent. You may know a fiction editor who can recommend a good nonfiction publisher.

CONTRACT TIP #2:

Even though larger publishers are usually looking for experienced authors, if you have a chance to talk with one of the "big boys" at a writers' conference, jump on it. It is not unheard-of for Zondervan, Thomas Nelson, and other big-name houses to publish a first-time author.

CONTRACT TIP #3:

Prepare a list of promotional possibilities for your publisher—potential connections that would be interested in hearing about your book. What are your local media outlets? Do you belong to any organizations? What about your hometown newspaper or website?

Appendix A

Checklist for Revision and Finalizing of Manuscript

____ Quoted material: Please provide credit information (author, title, city, publisher, date, page number) for all quoted material.

____ Lengthy quoted material: Permission must be obtained for use of longer material (more than a sentence or two, usually), and for poetry and song quotes of any length. (Please be aware that, by contract, any fees charged for use of quoted material must be paid by the author.)

____ Bible translation: Please identify what Bible translation you are using for quoted passages of Scripture. If you are using more than one, please identify the alternate translations. (We prefer that you limit your usage to no more than three translations, with one translation used the majority of the time.)

____ Typesetting issues: Are your hyphens, dashes, quotation marks, apostrophes, etc. correct? Check with your publisher on the preferred use of curly vs. straight quotation marks and apostrophes. Be sure you know when to use an em-dash, an en-dash, or a hyphen, and type those correctly into your manuscript.

____ Make sure opening quotation marks have closing marks (or we'll have to guess where the quote ends!) The same goes for parentheses—it's easy to forget to close a parenthetical comment.

____ Bible verse typesetting: Please be sure all quoted Bible verses are exactly as printed in the Bible version. For example, if the word "Lord" or "God" is in small caps (Lord, God) you need to type it in that manner as well. If a long passage has paragraph breaks or is set in separate lines like poetry (the Psalms and much of the Prophets are set this way in most translations), please type it in that way, unless your publisher advises otherwise.

____ Graphics: Do you have any illustrations or photos with the book? If so, please remove them from the word-processing file, and put them in separate, high-resolution graphics files.

____ Special elements: Are sidebars, quotes at start of chapters, captions, discussion questions, and other repeated elements clearly marked and consistently placed throughout manuscript?

____ Footnotes/endnotes: We encourage the use of endnotes rather than footnotes. Endnotes should be in a separate file, numbered consecutively by chapter. Please use superscripted numbers in the text of the book to indicate an endnote, like the "1" at the end of this sentence.[1] (Do not use your word processor's automated endnote program. The information in the endnote can be lost, because the automated endnotes do not translate over to the typesetting program.)

____ Text Boxes: Please take any text in boxes out of the boxes and put them the body of the manuscript.

Appendix B

Sample Permission Letter

(Replace words in brackets with the appropriate text)

[DATE]

[NAME, TITLE]

[COMPANY]

[ADDRESS]

[CITY, STATE, ZIP]

Dear [NAME]:

I am writing to request permission to quote a passage from one of your publications:

[TITLE], by [AUTHOR], [COPYRIGHT DATE], [PAGE NUMBER(S) BEING QUOTED]

A photocopy of the page(s) on which your material will appear is attached for your review. This material is being quoted in the following work being published by [PUBLISHER'S NAME, PUBLISHER'S CITY]:

[TITLE] by [AUTHOR]

Proposed date of publication: [MONTH, YEAR]

Format: [TRADE PAPER, MASS MARKET, HARDCOVER]

Price: $_____ (tentative)

Initial press run: _____ (tentative)

I request nonexclusive world rights, as part of this volume only, in all languages and for all editions for the life of the product. If you are not the copyright holder of this material, or additional permission is needed from another source, please so advise. Unless you request otherwise, we will include the standard bibliographic credit line, including publisher, author, title, etc.

Your earliest attention to this matter would be greatly appreciated, since my deadline for permissions is imminent. Please sign one copy of this letter and return it to me in the enclosed self-addressed, stamped envelope. In signing, you grant the permission requested above and warrant that you are the sole owner (or the owner's representative) of the rights granted herein, and that the material indicated does not infringe upon the copyright or other rights of any third party.

_____ Permission granted to use the material described above with a standard credit line.

_____ Permission granted to use the material described above with the following credit line: _____

_____

Name: _____

Title: _____

(Signed) _____

Date: _____

Thank you for your consideration.

_____, author

encl: photocopied text, second copy of this letter, SASE

Endnotes

Chapter 1

1. A.W. Tozer, *The Pursuit of Man* (Camp Hill, PA: Christian Publications, 1950, 1978), page xii.

2. Larry Libby, "Collecting Tools, Collecting Dust." *Moody*, Dec. 1993, pp. 14–16.

Chapter 3

1. Poll conducted in 2001 by George Barna (www.barna.org), cited in *Virtual Christian Magazine*, http://www.vcmagazine.org/article.aspx ?volume=3&issue=2&article=help.

Chapter 5

1. Laura Hillenbrand, interviewed by Michael Neff on WebdelSol. com.

Chapter 6

1. Dwight V. Swain, *Techniques of the Selling Writer* (Norman, OK: Univ. of Oklahoma Press, 1973), p. 35.

2. John Grisham, *Bleachers* (New York: Random House [paperback ed.], 2007), p. 133.

3. Gordon D. Fee and Douglas Stuart, *How to Read the Bible for All Its Worth* (Grand Rapids, MI: Zondervan, 2003).

4. Fred Hartley, *Holy Spirit, Fill Me!* (Camp Hill, PA: Christian Publications, 1992), p. 3.

Chapter 7

1. Giovanni Papini, *The Life of Christ*, trans. Dorothy Canfield Fisher (New York: Harcourt, Brace and Co., 1923), pp. 14–15.

2. Sir Arthur Quiller-Couch, *On the Art of Writing* (New York: G. P. Putnam's Sons, 1916), p. 281.

3. Arthur Bloch, *Murphy's Law, and Other Reasons Why Things Go WRONG* (London: Methuen Paperbacks Ltd., 1977), pp. 9–11.

Chapter 8

1. Jonathan Kirsch, *Kirsch's Handbook of Publishing Law* (Venice CA: Acrobat Books, 1995), p. 148.

2. University of Chicago Press, ed., *The Chicago Manual of Style, 15th Edition* (Chicago: University of Chicago Press, 2003).

3. Robert Hudson, *A Christian Writer's Manual of Style* (Grand Rapids, MI: Zondervan, 1988).

4. Leonard Goss and Carolyn Stanford Goss, *The Little Style Guide to Great Christian Writing and Publishing* (Nashville: Broadman & Holman, 2004).

Chapter 9

1. The author would like to thank attorney William Shumway for his advice on the wording of this section.

About the Author

David E. Fessenden is senior editor/acquisitions for CLC Publications, the U.S. publishing house for CLC Ministries International (formerly Christian Literature Crusade). Dave has a B.A. in journalism, an M.A. in religion, and over 25 years of experience in writing and editing. Before beginning his ministry with CLC, he launched an editorial consulting business after 12 years on the staff of Christian Publications, Inc., the majority of that time as managing editor. In previous positions Dave served on the communications staff of Elim Bible Institute and was editor of a regional edition of the largest Protestant weekly newspaper in the country.

Dave has published four books, produced study guides for two titles by A.W. Tozer (published in the back of the books), written hundreds of newspaper and magazine articles, and edited numerous books. He was a regular columnist for *Cross & Quill*, a Christian writers newsletter, and a frequent speaker at writers' conferences. Dave also conducts Sunday school teaching workshops based on his book, *Teaching with All Your Heart*.

Dave, and his wife Jacque, live in the Philadelphia area and have two adult sons.

Other Works by David Fessenden:

Father to Nobody's Children: the Story of Thomas J. Barnardo

Teaching with All Your Heart

The Waiting Missionary

A Light to All Japan (children's version)

Study guides for A.W. Tozer's Attributes of God, Vols. 1 & 2

Visit Dave's blog: fromconcepttocontract.com

Original Art by Ed Sabatino

**Click here via your Smart Phone
to visit Dave's online blog.**